LA GOMI

TRAVEL GUIDE 2026

Exploring the Hidden Charms of Spain's Canary Island

Monroe k. Shimmer

Copyright © by Monroe k. Shimmer
All rights reserved. No part of this publication may be reproduced, distributed, or transmitted in any form or by any means, including photocopying, recording, or other electronic or mechanical methods, without the prior written permission of the author, except in the case of brief quotations used in reviews or scholarly works.

LA GOMERA – MY JOURNEY, YOUR GUIDE

I still remember the first time I stepped off the ferry and felt the air of La Gomera wrap around me. It wasn't just warm—it was calm, almost like the island was whispering, *"Slow down, you're here now."* The ocean shimmered like a painting, the mountains rose up in gentle green waves, and the streets had this laid-back charm that made me forget the rush of everyday life.

I came here with a mix of excitement and curiosity. I had heard of La Gomera's beauty—the black sand beaches, the wild cliffs, the lush forests of Garajonay National Park—but no one told me just how magical it feels when you're standing in the middle of it all. I wandered through small villages where everyone seemed to know each other, tasted food so fresh it felt like it came straight from the earth, and listened to the soft, melodic whistling of *Silbo Gomero*, the island's unique language.

But here's the thing—I also got lost. I missed buses. I arrived at some viewpoints just as clouds rolled in. I found myself staring at closed restaurant doors because I didn't know their opening hours. And while those little mistakes became part of my adventure, I couldn't help but think—*what if there was a way to make this easier for other travelers?*

That's why I decided to write this book. Not just for people coming here for the first time, but also for those who have been before and want to discover what they might have missed. I want you to know where to find the quietest beaches, which trails will leave you speechless, the best times to visit each spot, and the little tips that locals shared with me over coffee or a glass of wine.

I've walked these streets, hiked these paths, and watched the sunsets from more places than I can count. I've made mistakes so you don't have to. I've found shortcuts, hidden gems, and the kind of experiences that photos can't fully capture. This book is my way of passing that on to you—so you can explore La Gomera without the stress, without wasting time, and with more moments to simply breathe it all in.

Because La Gomera isn't just a place you visit. It's a place you feel. And I want you to feel it in the best possible way.

Contents

La Gomera – My Journey, Your Guide 4

Introduction 10

    Why Visit La Gomera 10

    A Glimpse into Its History and Culture 12

    The Island's Unique Atmosphere and Pace of Life 14

Planning Your Trip 16

    Best Time to Visit 16

    How to Get There 18

    Getting Around the Island 20

    Budgeting for Your Trip 22

    Travel Tips and Local Etiquette 24

Geography and Regions 26

    Overview of La Gomera's Landscape 26

    Valle Gran Rey 27

    San Sebastián de La Gomera 29

    Hermigua 31

    Agulo 33

    Vallehermoso 35

    Playa Santiago 37

    Alajeró and Other Villages 39

Must-See Attractions – Island Highlights 41

    Garajonay National Park (UNESCO World Heritage Site) 41

    Alto de Garajonay Peak 43

    El Cedro Forest 45

    Mirador de Abrante (Glass Skywalk) 47

    Roque Agando 49

    Los Órganos Sea Cliffs (by Boat) 51

    Mirador de Igualero 53

    San Sebastián de La Gomera Historic Center 55

    Torre del Conde 56

    Church of the Assumption (Iglesia de la Asunción) 58

    Archaeological Museum of La Gomera 60

    Hermigua's Banana Plantations and El Pescante Ruins 62

    Agulo – "The Bonbon of La Gomera" 64

    Vallehermoso and Its Botanical Gardens 65

    Playa de Santiago's Fishing Village Charm 67

    Monumento Natural de Los Roques 69

Beaches and Coastal Escapes 71

    Playa de Vueltas 71

    Playa del Inglés (Black Sand Beauty) 73

    Playa de la Caleta 75

    Playa de Santiago 77

    Playa de Avalos 79

    Secluded Coves and Hidden Shores 81

Nature and Outdoor Activities 83

    Hiking in Garajonay National Park 83

    The GR-131 Long-Distance Trail 85

Whale and Dolphin Watching Excursions 87

Diving and Snorkeling Spots 89

Kayaking Along the Coast 91

Birdwatching in Valle Gran Rey 93

Cycling and Mountain Biking Routes 95

Where to Stay 97

Types of Accommodation 97

Popular Areas to Stay 99

Practical Tips for Booking and Choosing the Right Place 101

Food and Drink 103

Must-Try Dishes (Almogrote, Potaje de Berros, Fish Specialties)
.... 103

Best Restaurants in San Sebastián 105

Seafront Dining in Valle Gran Rey 107

Village Tapas Bars 109

Local Drinks and Desserts 111

Itineraries 114

One-Day Cruise Stop Highlights 114

3-Day Short Break 116

5-Day Nature and Culture Tour 119

7-Day Full Island Experience 122

Hiking-Focused Itinerary 125

Relaxation and Wellness Retreat Plan 128

Practical Information 131

Money and Currency 131
Safety and Emergency Contacts 133
Internet and Mobile Connectivity 135
Sustainable and Responsible Travel on La Gomera 137
Conclusion 139

INTRODUCTION

Why Visit La Gomera

When you think of the Canary Islands, places like Tenerife or Gran Canaria might come to mind first. But La Gomera is different. It is quieter, smaller, and feels untouched in a way that makes you slow down and breathe. You don't come here for crowded resorts or endless nightlife—you come here to reconnect with nature, discover hidden villages, and experience an island that still holds on to its traditions.

As soon as you arrive, you notice how unhurried life feels. The ferry from Tenerife sets the tone—leaving behind the busy ports, you glide across the Atlantic and step onto an island where time seems to move differently. La Gomera is not about rushing from one attraction to another. It is about walking old trails through ancient forests, sitting in a family-run restaurant where the owner brings you food straight from their kitchen, or standing at a viewpoint where the clouds float at your feet.

What makes La Gomera so special is its variety of landscapes packed into such a small space. In less than an hour, you can drive from the coast with its black sand beaches up to the misty heights of Garajonay National Park, where moss covers the trees and silence feels almost sacred. The island is full of dramatic contrasts: sunlit banana plantations in Hermigua, rugged cliffs that plunge into the sea at Agulo, and valleys painted green in every shade you can imagine.

La Gomera is also one of the best places for hiking in the Canary Islands. The network of trails here is remarkable, and whether you're a casual walker or a serious hiker, you'll find paths that lead you through forests, along ridges, and down into hidden ravines. Every step feels like an invitation to see a side of the island that cars cannot reach.

But it isn't just about nature. The culture here is rich and unique, from the whistling language of *Silbo Gomero*—still taught in schools—to the traditional dishes like *almogrote* and watercress soup that you won't find anywhere else. Festivals bring music, dance, and color to even the smallest villages, and the people you meet are warm, welcoming, and proud of their heritage.

Visiting La Gomera is like stepping into another rhythm of life. It gives you space to pause, to notice the sound of the ocean at night, the taste of fresh tropical fruit, or the view of Tenerife's Mount Teide rising above the horizon. It is a place that doesn't just impress you—it stays with you long after you leave.

That is why you visit La Gomera. Not for big resorts or tourist crowds, but for something far more valuable: peace, beauty, and the feeling that you've discovered a hidden world in the middle of the Atlantic.

A Glimpse into Its History and Culture

When you walk through La Gomera, you quickly realize that the island's charm is not only in its landscapes but also in its history and culture. Every village, every square, and every trail carries stories that connect the past with the present.

Long before Europeans arrived, the island was home to the indigenous Gomerans, who lived off the land and developed their own way of life. Even though much of their history was lost after the Spanish conquest in the 15th century, traces of their presence remain in archaeological sites and in traditions that have survived through time. One of the most unique is *Silbo Gomero*, the whistling language created to communicate across the island's deep ravines and valleys. Today it is recognized by UNESCO as part of the world's cultural heritage and is still taught in schools, making it one of the few living whistling languages in the world.

La Gomera also holds an important place in global history. In 1492, Christopher Columbus stopped here on his way to the Americas. In San Sebastián de La Gomera, you can still visit places tied to his stay, like the Torre del Conde and the Church of the Assumption. Standing in these sites, it's easy to imagine the ships anchored in the harbor and the sense of anticipation before that famous voyage began.

The island's culture has been shaped by its geography. With steep mountains and isolated valleys, communities grew close-knit and developed strong local traditions. Music and dance are an important part of life, often heard during festivals where drums and chants echo through the streets. Food also reflects this heritage, with dishes that are simple but full of flavor, made from what the land and sea provide. Eating *gofio* (a roasted grain flour), tasting *almogrote* (a cheese paste with peppers and garlic), or sipping local wine connects you directly to centuries of tradition.

Religion also plays a role in the cultural fabric of La Gomera. Small chapels and churches can be found across the island, often perched on hillsides or in village centers. Many of the island's festivals are linked to religious celebrations, mixing devotion with music, dancing, and food in a way that feels both spiritual and deeply communal.

What makes the culture of La Gomera so striking is how alive it still is. This isn't history locked away in museums—it's something you experience as you move through the island. You hear it in the whistles that carry across the valleys, you see it in the architecture of whitewashed houses with red-tiled roofs, and you feel it when locals welcome you with warmth and pride.

By exploring La Gomera's history and culture, you discover that this small island is not just a beautiful destination but also a place where the past and present live side by side, shaping an identity that is both unique and unforgettable.

The Island's Unique Atmosphere and Pace of Life

From the moment you set foot on La Gomera, you notice something different. The air feels cleaner, the sounds softer, and time seems to stretch in a way that makes you want to slow down. Unlike other destinations where you might feel the pressure to see and do everything quickly, La Gomera invites you to take your time and let the island reveal itself at its own rhythm.

Life here moves gently. Villages are small, streets are quiet, and people are never in a rush. You'll see locals sitting in shaded squares, sipping coffee, or chatting with neighbors as though the day has no end. Shops close for siesta, meals linger longer, and even the ocean seems to roll in with a calmer tide. It doesn't take long before you find yourself adjusting to this slower pace, realizing that there is no need to hurry.

The island's atmosphere is deeply tied to its landscapes. When you walk through the misty forests of Garajonay, there is a sense of peace that makes you want to whisper instead of talk. Standing at a cliffside viewpoint with the wind on your face, you feel small in the best possible way, as though the island is reminding you to just be present. Even in the more lively areas, like Valle Gran Rey, the energy is relaxed, with beachside cafés where time seems to pass unnoticed.

This unique pace of life is one of La Gomera's greatest treasures. It allows you to notice things you might overlook elsewhere—the sound of birds calling across a valley, the smell of fresh bread from a village bakery, the sight of stars stretching across the night sky without city lights to dim them. Instead of rushing to tick off attractions, you find yourself living each moment fully, whether it's sharing a simple meal, watching the sunset, or wandering through narrow village streets.

For travelers, this atmosphere can feel like a reset. It's a chance to step away from stress, noise, and schedules, and to reconnect with a way of life that values presence over speed. La Gomera doesn't demand much from you—only that you slow down enough to feel its rhythm. And once you do, you carry a little piece of that calm with you, long after you've left the island.

PLANNING YOUR TRIP

Best Time to Visit

La Gomera has a mild climate throughout the year, which means you can visit almost any time and still enjoy good weather. The island sits in the Atlantic, just off the coast of Africa, so its temperatures rarely swing to extremes. Winters are gentle, with cool evenings but plenty of sunshine during the day, while summers are warm without being unbearably hot thanks to the ocean breeze.

If you prefer hiking, spring and autumn are perfect seasons to come. From March to May, the island turns green with wildflowers blooming across the valleys, and the temperatures make long walks through Garajonay National Park very comfortable. September to November is also ideal, as the summer heat fades but the sea is still warm enough for swimming, and the crowds are much smaller. These months let you enjoy both the coast and the mountains in balance.

Summer, from June to August, is the busiest period, especially in Valle Gran Rey and the coastal villages. Days are longer, the sea is inviting, and the atmosphere is lively with visitors arriving from other Canary Islands and mainland Spain. If you enjoy a more social vibe and want plenty of beach time, this season is for you, though it is wise to book accommodation early.

Winter, between December and February, is the calmest season. While northern Europe is cold, La Gomera enjoys mild days that attract those looking for sunshine and peace. It's the best time to escape the winter blues, but you should be prepared for cooler evenings and the chance of mist or rain in the higher parts of the island. On clear days, winter skies often give you the sharpest views of Mount Teide rising from Tenerife.

Festivals can also play a role in choosing when to visit. Local celebrations take place all year, with colorful processions, traditional music, and village gatherings that bring the culture of the island to life. Planning your trip to coincide with one of these events can make your experience even more memorable.

How to Get There

Getting to La Gomera is part of the adventure, because the island feels just far enough from the rest of the world to stay special, yet close enough to reach without much difficulty. There is no international airport here, so you won't find direct flights from other countries, but that is part of its charm. You arrive knowing that this place is a little hidden, a little protected, and that makes it even more rewarding once you get here.

The most common way to reach La Gomera is by ferry from Tenerife. Ferries leave several times a day from Los Cristianos in the south of Tenerife, and the crossing takes just under an hour. You can travel as a foot passenger or bring a car with you if you plan to drive around the island. On clear days, the trip itself is beautiful, with views of Mount Teide behind you and La Gomera's rugged coast growing larger ahead. Both Fred Olsen and Naviera Armas operate regular services, and tickets can be booked online or at the port. It's worth checking schedules in advance because sailing times can vary depending on the season.

If you prefer to fly, La Gomera does have a small airport near Playa Santiago. Flights connect the island with Tenerife North Airport and Gran Canaria, usually with short journeys of around half an hour. This is the fastest option if you are already in the Canary Islands and want to skip the ferry. The airport is small and easy to navigate, and car rentals are available right outside.

Another way travelers often arrive is by cruise ship. San Sebastián de La Gomera is a popular stop for cruises exploring the Canary Islands or Atlantic routes. If you arrive this way, you'll find the town center just a short walk from the port, which makes it easy to explore even if you only have a day on the island.

Whichever option you choose, the journey is smooth and well-organized. The island may feel remote, but connections are regular and reliable. Once you arrive, you'll notice how quickly the pace changes—from the busier feel of Tenerife or Gran Canaria to the calm, unhurried rhythm of La Gomera. The trip is not just about reaching your destination, but also about the sense of escape that begins as soon as you set out toward the island.

Getting Around the Island

Once you arrive in La Gomera, the question becomes how to explore it. The island may be small, but its steep valleys, twisting roads, and hidden corners mean that getting around requires a bit of planning. The good news is that whether you choose to drive, take public transport, or rely on your own two feet, there is always a way to see the best of what the island has to offer.

The easiest and most flexible option is to hire a car. Driving gives you the freedom to stop at viewpoints, reach remote villages, and set your own pace. The roads are well-maintained, but they are also winding, with plenty of sharp bends as they climb into the mountains. For some people, this is part of the thrill, as every turn opens up to another spectacular view. Car rental agencies can be found at the airport, in San Sebastián, and in some of the larger towns. If you are planning to visit many places in a short amount of time, having your own car will save you hours compared to waiting for buses.

If driving isn't for you, the island has a reliable network of public buses, known locally as *guaguas*. They connect the main towns and villages, though the schedules are not as frequent as in bigger islands. Buses are a good option if you are staying in one place and planning day trips, but you'll need to check timetables carefully and be ready for slower journeys. On the plus side, bus rides give you the chance to sit back and take in the scenery without worrying about the roads.

Hiking is another way to move around, and in La Gomera it is more than just a mode of transport—it is an experience in itself. The island is famous for its extensive trail network, many of which follow ancient paths once used by locals to move between villages.

Walking here brings you close to the land in a way that driving never can. You'll find trails that take you from the coast up into Garajonay National Park, through deep ravines, and across ridges with unforgettable views. For shorter distances, walking is often the most direct way to reach beaches, farms, or viewpoints that roads cannot access.

Taxis are also available in the main towns and can be a useful backup if you miss a bus or want a quicker way back after a long hike. Some taxi drivers even offer tours of the island, combining convenience with local knowledge.

Budgeting for Your Trip

Planning your budget for La Gomera is not just about setting limits—it's about making sure you can enjoy everything the island has to offer without unnecessary stress. The good news is that La Gomera can fit different types of travelers, whether you are looking for comfort or prefer a simpler and more affordable experience.

Your biggest expenses will usually be accommodation, food, and transportation. Hotels, guesthouses, and rural cottages are spread across the island, with prices ranging from budget-friendly rooms to more luxurious stays. If you want to save, you'll find small family-run pensions or apartments where you can cook your own meals. On the other hand, if comfort is important, boutique hotels and resorts offer packages with meals and extras included.

Eating out in La Gomera can also be adapted to your budget. Local cafés and restaurants often serve hearty dishes at reasonable prices, especially if you stick to the menus of the day. Traditional Canarian food like *almogrote* or fresh fish is both delicious and affordable. If you shop in local markets or small supermarkets, you can prepare your own meals for even less.

Transport is another part of your budget. Renting a car is the most flexible option, but it is also one of the more expensive choices once you add fuel and insurance. Public buses cost much less, though you'll trade convenience for savings. Hiking, of course, is free, aside from the cost of good shoes and perhaps a guidebook or app.

Activities on the island range from free experiences, like walking through Garajonay National Park or exploring small villages, to paid ones, such as guided tours, boat trips, or cultural events. Many of the natural attractions don't cost anything, which makes La Gomera kinder to your wallet compared to larger, busier destinations.

When planning, it's wise to set aside some extra money for unexpected things—like discovering a restaurant you can't resist, buying handmade crafts, or joining a last-minute dolphin-watching excursion. These little moments often become the highlights of your trip.

Overall, La Gomera doesn't demand a fortune to enjoy fully. With a bit of planning, you can balance comfort with adventure, keeping your trip affordable while still leaving space for a few indulgences.

Travel Tips and Local Etiquette

Traveling through La Gomera feels easy once you get into the rhythm of the island, but knowing a few tips and customs will help you blend in and make your experience smoother. Life here moves at a slower pace than in many other places, so the first thing to remember is patience. Shops, restaurants, and services may not always run on a strict schedule, and people value enjoying the moment rather than rushing.

When it comes to greetings, a simple "hola" with a smile goes a long way. Locals are warm and friendly, and showing basic courtesy makes interactions much easier. If you are invited to someone's home or you spend time in smaller villages, a handshake or even the traditional kiss on both cheeks is common. Respecting personal space and being polite in conversation is important, especially with older generations.

Dining customs are also worth noting. Meals are often slower and more social, so don't expect quick service or rushed eating. Lunch is usually the biggest meal of the day, and dinner tends to be later in the evening. If you are eating in a traditional restaurant, try to enjoy local dishes without asking for too many changes, as food is served the way it is meant to be prepared. Tipping is not required but rounding up the bill or leaving some coins is always appreciated.

On the road, be cautious and respectful. Many of the roads in La Gomera are narrow, winding, and steep. Locals drive with skill but also expect attention and courtesy from other drivers. If you are renting a car, take your time, let faster drivers pass, and always park responsibly, especially in the smaller towns where space is limited.

In nature, respect is essential. La Gomera is known for its pristine landscapes, especially Garajonay National Park. Stay on marked trails, don't pick plants, and avoid leaving any litter. Silence and calm are part of the island's character, so keeping noise levels low helps preserve the atmosphere that makes this place so special.

Finally, remember that La Gomera is not just a holiday spot but a home to its people. Supporting local businesses, buying handmade crafts, or eating in family-owned restaurants not only enriches your experience but also gives back to the community. By respecting traditions and embracing the island's slower lifestyle, you'll find that your time here becomes much more rewarding.

GEOGRAPHY AND REGIONS

Overview of La Gomera's Landscape

La Gomera may be small, but its landscape is incredibly dramatic and full of contrasts. As soon as you set foot on the island, you notice how different it feels from its neighbors in the Canary Islands. The coastline is rugged, with steep cliffs that drop into the Atlantic Ocean, while deep valleys cut into the land, creating hidden villages and fertile terraces where bananas, grapes, and palms grow.

The center of the island is dominated by Garajonay National Park, a lush green world of ancient laurel forest that often feels like stepping back in time. Mist from the clouds keeps this part of La Gomera cool and damp, creating an almost magical atmosphere. Walking through the forest trails, you'll hear the sound of birds and flowing streams rather than the noise of city life.

In contrast, the lower slopes and coastlines are drier and sunnier. Here, you find black sand beaches, volcanic rock formations, and small towns that hug the shores. The sharp changes in altitude mean that within just a short drive, you can go from a cool, misty forest to a sunny beach.

La Gomera's shape adds to its unique beauty. Seen from above, the island looks like a giant green dome cut with deep ravines called "barrancos." These ravines spread outward like the spokes of a wheel, making travel both exciting and adventurous. The views from the higher points are breathtaking, with the blue Atlantic stretching endlessly and, on clear days, Tenerife's Mount Teide rising in the distance.

Valle Gran Rey

Valle Gran Rey is one of the most popular and picturesque areas of La Gomera, yet it manages to keep a relaxed, almost bohemian vibe. As soon as you arrive, you'll notice the terraces of banana plantations cascading down the hills, the small white houses clinging to the slopes, and the deep green of the surrounding mountains meeting the blue Atlantic. The valley stretches along the coast, with several beaches that vary from lively to quiet, each offering a slightly different experience.

When you explore Valle Gran Rey, there is plenty to see and do. Walking along the main promenade, you can stop at local cafés or small restaurants to taste fresh fish, tropical fruit, and local specialties. The beaches are perfect for sunbathing, swimming, or just sitting and enjoying the sound of the waves. If you enjoy hiking, there are trails that take you up the hills and through the nearby ravines, providing breathtaking views over the valley and the ocean. Some of these trails continue into Garajonay National Park for longer hikes, allowing you to experience the island's lush interior.

The town itself has a charming mix of old and new. You'll find small shops selling handmade crafts and local products, along with art galleries and spaces where you can see local culture up close. Music and street performances sometimes appear in the evenings, giving a lively but relaxed atmosphere that draws both locals and visitors. If you enjoy a slower pace, you can wander into the smaller villages within the valley, such as La Calera or La Playa, and discover quiet corners, hidden viewpoints, and terraces perfect for watching the sunset.

Valle Gran Rey is very accessible, with roads leading from San Sebastián de La Gomera and connections to other northern villages.

Accommodation ranges from simple guesthouses to boutique hotels and apartments. The beaches are free to access, and parking is usually available nearby, though it can be limited in the busier season. The valley is also well served by public buses, but having a car allows you to explore the surrounding hills and viewpoints at your own pace.

San Sebastián de La Gomera

San Sebastián de La Gomera is the island's capital and its main gateway, giving you a mix of history, culture, and coastal charm. As soon as you step off the ferry or arrive at the small airport, you feel the town's unique energy—a combination of quiet island life and the subtle buzz of a working port. The streets are narrow and winding, lined with whitewashed houses with red-tiled roofs, flower-filled balconies, and small shops that invite you to explore.

The town is full of history, with several sites that connect you to the island's past. The Torre del Conde, a stone tower built in the 15th century, stands as a reminder of the island's defensive history and offers a small but fascinating insight into the era of early Spanish settlements. Nearby, the Church of the Assumption holds both religious and cultural significance, and stepping inside gives you a sense of how life on the island has evolved over centuries. Walking through the town, you will notice the influence of the Gomeran and Spanish heritage in architecture, street layouts, and local customs.

Exploring San Sebastián is as much about atmosphere as it is about sightseeing. The harbor area is lively, with fishing boats, ferries, and occasional cruise ships adding motion to the calm surroundings. Along the waterfront, you can enjoy a fresh seafood meal while watching the Atlantic waves, or simply take a stroll and absorb the town's relaxed energy. Local markets and shops give you the chance to pick up handcrafted items, local produce, and souvenirs that reflect the island's culture.

For practical information, the town is compact and easy to navigate on foot. Most of the historic sites and main streets are within walking distance of the ferry port. Public buses connect San Sebastián to other towns and villages across the island, and taxis are readily available if you want quicker access to more remote areas. The town is open year-round, and while shops and restaurants may close briefly during siesta hours, you'll find enough activity to explore comfortably throughout the day.

Hermigua

Hermigua is a peaceful valley town on the northern coast of La Gomera, known for its lush landscapes and laid-back atmosphere. As you arrive, you'll immediately notice the steep hillsides covered in banana plantations and the winding roads that lead down to the small black sand beaches. The combination of green terraces, the Atlantic Ocean, and the surrounding mountains gives Hermigua a calm and refreshing vibe, perfect for anyone looking to slow down and connect with nature.

Exploring Hermigua offers a mix of nature, culture, and quiet village life. You can wander through the town's narrow streets lined with traditional white houses, stopping at cafés or small shops to try local products like honey, gofio, and tropical fruit. The town is surrounded by excellent hiking routes, some of which take you up into Garajonay National Park or along the coastline with breathtaking views over the ocean. Vallehermoso, nearby, can also be reached from Hermigua by scenic walking paths if you enjoy a longer trek.

One of the highlights of Hermigua is its natural pools and small beaches, where you can relax or take a swim in calm waters. The area is less crowded than other parts of the island, giving you a sense of privacy and escape. You might also discover small viewpoints that overlook the valley and the sea, providing picture-perfect moments without the need for a guide.

Hermigua is easy to reach by car, with roads connecting it to San Sebastián de La Gomera, Agulo, and Valle Gran Rey. Public buses serve the area, though schedules are limited, so having a vehicle or planning your time carefully is helpful. Accommodation options range from small rural hotels and guesthouses to vacation apartments, many of which offer terraces with stunning views over the valley. Local restaurants and cafés are open most of the day, though some close for siesta, so timing meals appropriately can help you make the most of your visit.

Agulo

Agulo is often called one of the most picturesque villages in La Gomera, and stepping into it feels like stepping back in time. Perched on a hillside overlooking the Atlantic Ocean, the village is famous for its narrow cobbled streets, whitewashed houses, and colorful flower-filled balconies. The charm of Agulo is immediate; it's quiet, inviting, and offers some of the best views on the island.

Exploring Agulo, you'll find several things that make it special. The town itself is perfect for wandering, discovering hidden squares, small cafés, and local shops selling handcrafted products. There are several viewpoints just a short walk from the village center, such as Mirador de Abrante, where the cliffs drop dramatically into the ocean below. From here, on a clear day, you can see Tenerife rising above the horizon, and the panorama is simply unforgettable.

Agulo is also a starting point for some of the island's most rewarding hikes. Trails lead up into Garajonay National Park or down through the ravines toward the coast, allowing you to experience both the lush interior and the dramatic coastline. Walking these paths gives you a real sense of the island's diversity, from misty forests to sun-soaked terraces and cliffs.

The village is small and easy to navigate on foot. You'll find a handful of restaurants offering local Canarian dishes, and their terraces often overlook the valley and the ocean, making every meal a scenic experience. Accommodation options are limited but charming, including small guesthouses and rural apartments that offer a quiet retreat with amazing views.

Agulo is accessible by car from San Sebastián de La Gomera, Hermigua, and other northern towns. Public buses also stop here, but services can be infrequent, so planning is recommended if you are not driving. Visiting is free, but some viewpoints may have small entry fees if they are privately managed, such as the glass platform at Mirador de Abrante, which enhances the experience of standing above the cliffs.

Vallehermoso

Vallehermoso is a charming town tucked into the northwestern part of La Gomera, and its name, which means "beautiful valley," perfectly captures its essence. Surrounded by lush mountains, fertile terraces, and the deep blue of the Atlantic in the distance, the town offers a peaceful, authentic island experience. As you arrive, you'll notice the calm pace of life, the whitewashed houses, and the small squares that invite you to pause and take in the scenery.

Exploring Vallehermoso, you'll find a combination of natural beauty and cultural charm. The town itself is perfect for wandering on foot. You can stroll through quiet streets, discover small cafés and shops, and enjoy the view of the valley from one of the several terraces or lookouts scattered around the town. Vallehermoso is also surrounded by excellent hiking opportunities, with trails leading into Garajonay National Park or down to the coast, allowing you to experience both the misty forests and the dramatic cliffs along the ocean.

One of the highlights of Vallehermoso is its agricultural landscape. Walking through the town and surrounding areas, you'll see terraces full of bananas, grapes, and other crops that have been cultivated here for centuries. This connection to the land gives the area a feeling of authenticity and provides excellent opportunities for photography or simply enjoying the colors and textures of the valley.

For practical information, Vallehermoso is accessible by car from San Sebastián de La Gomera, Hermigua, and other northern towns. Public buses serve the town, though schedules are limited, so planning your route is recommended. Accommodation options include small hotels, guesthouses, and rural apartments, many with terraces overlooking the valley. Local restaurants serve traditional Canarian cuisine, and prices are generally reasonable. Walking around the town is easy, and parking is available near the main streets.

Playa Santiago

Playa Santiago is a small coastal town on the southern side of La Gomera, offering a quiet and authentic experience away from the busier tourist spots. As you arrive, you'll notice the charm of the harbor, the small fishing boats bobbing on the waves, and the promenade lined with cafés and restaurants where you can enjoy fresh seafood while listening to the gentle sound of the Atlantic. The black sand beach stretches along the coast, providing a peaceful spot to relax, swim, or simply watch the sunset.

Exploring Playa Santiago, you'll find a mix of laid-back beach life and access to natural beauty. Walking along the waterfront, you can stop to admire the fishing boats or explore small shops offering local crafts and produce. The surrounding hills and valleys provide hiking opportunities, with trails that take you through terraces, past banana plantations, and up to viewpoints overlooking the ocean. The town is also a convenient base for exploring other southern parts of the island, including the hiking paths that lead to more remote beaches or the interior of Garajonay National Park.

The town has a friendly and relaxed atmosphere. It is smaller than Valle Gran Rey, making it easy to wander on foot and enjoy the quiet streets and waterfront. Restaurants here serve fresh, locally caught fish and traditional Canarian dishes, and prices are generally reasonable. Accommodation ranges from small hotels and guesthouses to self-catering apartments, many offering terraces with views over the ocean or the surrounding hills.

Playa Santiago is accessible by car from San Sebastián de La Gomera and other parts of the island, with parking available near the harbor and beach. Public buses also connect the town to major villages, though schedules can be limited. The town is especially quiet outside of the peak summer months, making it ideal if you are seeking a slower pace and a more intimate connection with the island's southern coast.

Alajeró and Other Villages

Alajeró is a quiet town located on the southwestern coast of La Gomera, offering a more off-the-beaten-path experience compared to the busier tourist areas. As you arrive, you'll notice the calm streets, the small houses with traditional Canarian architecture, and the sense of community that makes the town feel welcoming. It is an ideal place to experience local life and enjoy the slower pace of the island.

Exploring Alajeró, you can stroll through the town's streets, visit small shops, and stop at cafés or local eateries to taste fresh seafood and regional specialties. The town serves as a gateway to the surrounding hills and valleys, providing access to hiking trails that lead to panoramic viewpoints or hidden beaches along the coast. Alajeró also has a charming harbor where you can watch fishing boats come and go, and even try a local boat tour or excursion.

Other small villages around the island, such as Chipude, Arure, and Las Hayas, each offer their own unique character. Chipude, perched in the interior, is known for its cultural festivals and traditional architecture, while Arure provides a glimpse into the rural life of La Gomera with its narrow streets and agricultural terraces. Las Hayas, close to Garajonay National Park, is perfect if you want to stay near the forest and enjoy hiking directly from your accommodation. Visiting these smaller villages allows you to see a side of La Gomera that is deeply authentic and often overlooked by visitors who only stick to the coast.

Alajeró and the surrounding villages are accessible by car, with roads connecting them to San Sebastián de La Gomera, Playa Santiago, and other parts of the island. Public buses serve some of the villages, though schedules can be limited, so driving or arranging transportation in advance is recommended. Accommodation options vary from small rural guesthouses to holiday apartments, often with terraces or gardens offering stunning views of the coast and valleys.

Spending time in Alajeró and the other villages gives you a sense of La Gomera beyond the main tourist hubs. It's a chance to enjoy tranquility, explore traditional ways of life, and discover hidden corners that make the island so special. These villages show the heart of La Gomera, where the beauty of the landscape and the charm of the people combine to create unforgettable experiences.

MUST-SEE ATTRACTIONS – ISLAND HIGHLIGHTS

Garajonay National Park (UNESCO World Heritage Site)

Garajonay National Park is the crown jewel of La Gomera and a must-visit destination for anyone exploring the island. Covering nearly a third of La Gomera, this UNESCO World Heritage Site protects one of Europe's last remaining laurel forests, an ancient ecosystem that has existed for millions of years. The park's thick, green canopy, mist-covered valleys, and moss-laden trees create a mystical atmosphere that feels entirely separate from the modern world. Walking here, you will sense the depth of history in every tree and the tranquility of an environment that has remained largely untouched.

When you explore Garajonay, there is an abundance of trails to choose from, ranging from short walks to full-day hikes. The Alto de Garajonay, the highest point on the island, offers sweeping panoramic views on clear days, allowing you to see across La Gomera and even to Tenerife with Mount Teide rising in the distance. El Cedro Forest is another highlight, with ancient trees, streams, and a sense of serenity that invites you to slow down and simply breathe in the natural beauty. Laguna Grande serves as a convenient starting point, offering easy trails, picnic areas, and the park's visitor center where you can learn about the forest's flora, fauna, and history.

Practical details make visiting Garajonay simple and accessible. The park is open year-round, and entrance is free, making it one of the easiest and most rewarding natural attractions on the island. The main visitor center near La Palmita typically operates from 9:30 in the morning until 4:30 in the afternoon, but it's wise to confirm times locally. Trails are accessible at all hours, though mornings are ideal because the light filtering through the trees is particularly beautiful, and the air is cooler.

Reaching the park is straightforward by car, with roads from San Sebastián, Valle Gran Rey, and Playa Santiago leading into various entrances. Parking is available near popular trailheads. If you rely on public transport, buses connect the major towns to some sections of the park, but schedules are limited, so plan ahead. Comfortable walking shoes are essential, and a light jacket is recommended, as the weather can change quickly and mist or rain is common, even on sunny days.

Visiting Garajonay National Park is more than just a hike; it's an immersion in a living forest that feels both ancient and alive. It's a place to slow down, appreciate the island's natural heritage, and experience one of the most unique landscapes in Europe. No trip to La Gomera is complete without spending time here.

Alto de Garajonay Peak

Alto de Garajonay is the highest point on La Gomera, rising 1,487 meters above sea level, and visiting it is a must for anyone who loves breathtaking views and dramatic landscapes. Standing at the summit, you'll feel a sense of awe as the island stretches beneath you in all directions. On clear days, you can see the deep green valleys, the rugged coastline, and even Mount Teide on Tenerife in the distance. The sense of being above the entire island is exhilarating and gives you a perspective on La Gomera that is impossible to experience anywhere else.

The peak is accessible via several hiking trails from different parts of Garajonay National Park. For a shorter and easier option, a trail from Laguna Grande or nearby visitor centers takes you through moss-covered laurel forests and past small streams, gradually climbing to the summit. The journey is as rewarding as the destination, with each step offering a new view of the forest canopy, the surrounding ridges, and the occasional glimpse of wildlife. For more experienced hikers, longer trails provide a full-day adventure through the heart of the park, combining dense forest, panoramic viewpoints, and the sense of solitude that makes Garajonay so special.

At the summit, there is a small monument marking the peak, and plenty of space to rest, take photos, and absorb the scenery. The air is often cooler than in the valleys below, and mist or clouds can appear suddenly, adding to the mystical atmosphere. It's important to dress in layers, wear sturdy shoes, and bring water, especially if you plan to hike from a more distant starting point.

Practical details make visiting the peak straightforward. There is no entrance fee, and the peak is accessible year-round, though weather conditions can affect visibility, so it's best to go on clear days if you want the full view. Parking is available at nearby trailheads for those arriving by car, and public buses connect the park's main points, though service is limited. The hike is manageable for most visitors with moderate fitness, but the terrain can be steep and uneven in parts, so take your time and enjoy the surroundings.

Visiting Alto de Garajonay gives you an unforgettable experience of La Gomera's natural beauty. It's a place to feel the vastness of the island, appreciate the ancient laurel forests below, and experience a perspective that few other spots can offer. Standing at the highest point, you'll understand why this island is so treasured by both locals and travelers alike.

El Cedro Forest

El Cedro Forest is one of the most enchanting corners of Garajonay National Park, and stepping into it feels like entering a different world. The forest is thick with ancient laurel trees, ferns, and moss-covered rocks, and a constant mist often drifts through the canopy, creating an atmosphere that is both peaceful and mysterious. As you walk through the forest, you'll notice the quiet hum of nature—birds singing, small streams trickling, and the soft crunch of leaves beneath your feet.

Exploring El Cedro, you'll find trails that range from short, gentle walks to longer hikes that take you deep into the forest. These paths are perfect for anyone who wants to experience the heart of La Gomera's unique ecosystem. The trails often lead to viewpoints where you can glimpse the surrounding mountains and valleys, giving a sense of the forest's vastness. Along the way, you might discover the endemic flora and fauna, some of which exist only on this island, making every step a chance to connect with the rare natural beauty of La Gomera.

One of the highlights of visiting El Cedro is the tranquility it offers. Unlike some parts of the park, which may attract larger groups, this forest often feels quiet and secluded, allowing you to fully immerse yourself in the environment. It's a perfect place to pause, take photographs, or simply breathe in the fresh, cool air. The soft mist and filtered sunlight give the forest a timeless quality, making it easy to understand why Garajonay is a UNESCO World Heritage Site.

Practical details make planning your visit simple. El Cedro is accessible by car from the main roads leading through Garajonay National Park, with parking available at trailheads. Entrance is free, and the forest can be explored year-round. Early mornings are ideal for visiting because the light is gentle, the air is fresh, and wildlife is often more active. Comfortable shoes, a light jacket, and water are recommended, as the forest floor can be damp and uneven.

Mirador de Abrante (Glass Skywalk)

Mirador de Abrante is one of La Gomera's most striking viewpoints, offering an experience that combines breathtaking scenery with a touch of adrenaline. Perched on the cliffs above the northern coast near the village of Agulo, the viewpoint features a glass skywalk that extends out over the edge, allowing you to look straight down to the valley and ocean below. The view from this height is spectacular, stretching across deep ravines, lush terraces, and the endless blue of the Atlantic. On clear days, you can even spot Tenerife rising in the distance, crowned by the summit of Mount Teide.

When you visit Mirador de Abrante, take time to explore the terrace and enjoy the panoramic vistas from different angles. Walking out on the glass platform gives you a thrilling perspective and an unforgettable photo opportunity. The viewpoint also features a small café where you can enjoy a coffee or snack while taking in the scenery, making it a perfect spot to pause and absorb the beauty of La Gomera. The surrounding area is ideal for a short walk, giving you glimpses of the village of Agulo and its charming streets nestled into the hillside.

Practical details are straightforward. There is a small entrance fee to access the glass skywalk, which helps maintain the facilities. The viewpoint is generally open daily, and visiting in the morning or late afternoon provides the best light for photos and the clearest views. The site is accessible by car from Agulo, with parking available nearby, and it can also be reached via local taxi or tour services. Comfortable shoes are recommended if you plan to explore the surrounding walking paths, and a light jacket may be useful as it can be windy at the cliff edge.

Visiting Mirador de Abrante is more than just seeing a view; it is an experience that mixes natural beauty, architecture, and a hint of adventure. Standing on the glass platform and looking down into the valley gives you a sense of La Gomera's dramatic landscape and the scale of its steep cliffs, making it an unforgettable stop for anyone exploring the northern part of the island.

Roque Agando

Roque Agando is one of La Gomera's most iconic natural landmarks, a massive volcanic rock rising dramatically from the heart of the island. Its sheer cliffs and distinctive shape make it instantly recognizable, and it is often seen as a symbol of the island's rugged beauty. As you approach, you'll be struck by the contrast between the dark, towering rock and the surrounding green valleys, which creates a dramatic and unforgettable scene.

Exploring Roque Agando involves both appreciation from a distance and closer hiking experiences. While the rock itself is protected and climbing it is not permitted, there are several trails nearby that allow you to walk around its base, offering different angles and panoramic views. The paths wind through lush laurel forests and across open hillsides, providing a mix of shaded and sunlit scenery. Photographers will find countless opportunities to capture the rock from various perspectives, especially during sunrise or sunset when the light casts dramatic shadows across the cliffs.

Practical details make visiting Roque Agando easy. The area is accessible by car from the main roads through the central part of La Gomera, with parking available near the main viewpoints. There is no entrance fee, and the site is open year-round. Comfortable shoes are recommended, as the terrain can be uneven, and bringing water is advised if you plan to hike around the area. The weather at higher altitudes can be cooler and windier than on the coast, so a light jacket or sweater is helpful, even on warmer days.

Visiting Roque Agando gives you a sense of the island's volcanic origins and its dramatic, rugged landscapes. It is a place to pause, take in the scale of nature, and appreciate the contrast between the massive rock formation and the green valleys surrounding it. For anyone exploring La Gomera, Roque Agando is a must-see landmark that captures the island's raw beauty and timeless character.

Los Órganos Sea Cliffs (by Boat)

The Los Órganos Sea Cliffs are one of La Gomera's most dramatic coastal sights, and the best way to experience them is from the water. Rising vertically from the Atlantic Ocean, these cliffs resemble the pipes of a giant organ, giving them their name. Their sheer scale and unique formations make them a truly unforgettable sight, and approaching them by boat adds a sense of adventure and perspective that you simply cannot get from the land.

When you take a boat tour to see Los Órganos, you'll glide along the coastline and witness the cliffs from different angles. The rock formations vary in color and shape, with volcanic textures that tell the story of the island's geological history. Seabirds often circle overhead, adding life to the scene, and on some tours, you might spot dolphins swimming alongside the boat, enhancing the sense of connection to nature. The boat tours typically provide commentary, explaining the formation of the cliffs, the surrounding marine life, and the history of the coast, which helps you fully appreciate what you are seeing.

Practical details are important for planning your visit. Tours usually depart from Playa Santiago, where several local operators run trips ranging from one to three hours. Prices vary depending on the length and type of tour, and it's recommended to book in advance during the busy season. The sea can be rough at times, so bring motion sickness medication if you are prone to it, and wear comfortable clothing and sunscreen. Morning tours often offer calmer waters and better lighting for photography, while afternoon trips can provide spectacular sunset views against the cliffs.

Visiting Los Órganos by boat gives you a unique perspective of La Gomera's rugged coastline and showcases the power and beauty of the Atlantic Ocean. Floating near the cliffs, surrounded by soaring rocks and open water, you'll feel the scale and drama of the island's natural environment. It's an experience that combines sightseeing, adventure, and a deep appreciation for the raw beauty that makes La Gomera so special.

Mirador de Igualero

Mirador de Igualero is one of the most spectacular viewpoints in La Gomera, offering breathtaking panoramas over Valle Gran Rey and the surrounding mountains. From this vantage point, you can see the terraced valleys descending toward the ocean, the scattered villages, and the deep ravines that give the landscape its dramatic character. The view is especially striking during sunrise or sunset, when the light transforms the hills and valleys into a tapestry of colors.

Visiting Mirador de Igualero allows you to enjoy more than just the scenery. There are walking paths nearby that let you explore the hillside and discover smaller viewpoints, hidden spots, and natural terraces. It's a perfect location for photography, picnicking, or simply pausing to take in the beauty of the valley and ocean. From here, you can also plan hikes down into Valle Gran Rey or explore other nearby trails that wind through banana plantations and traditional villages.

Practical details make this viewpoint easy to access. Mirador de Igualero is reachable by car from Valle Gran Rey, with parking available near the viewpoint. There is no entrance fee, and the site is open year-round. Comfortable shoes are recommended if you want to explore the surrounding paths, and a light jacket is useful as the altitude can bring cooler breezes even on sunny days. Visiting in the morning or late afternoon provides the best lighting for photography and the clearest views of the valley below.

Mirador de Igualero is a place to pause and appreciate the scale and beauty of La Gomera's landscapes. Standing at the edge of the viewpoint, looking out over the terraced valleys, villages, and ocean beyond, you gain a real sense of the island's dramatic topography and the harmony between nature and local life. It's a must-visit spot for anyone exploring Valle Gran Rey and the northern part of the island.

San Sebastián de La Gomera Historic Center

San Sebastián de La Gomera's historic center is the cultural heart of the island, where cobbled streets, whitewashed houses, and centuries-old architecture come together to tell the story of La Gomera's past. As you walk through the narrow lanes, you can almost feel the history beneath your feet, from the colonial-era buildings to the small squares where locals gather and children play. The charm of the area lies not just in its architecture, but in the atmosphere—calm, inviting, and authentically Canarian.

Exploring the historic center, you will find several points of interest. The Torre del Conde, a 15th-century stone tower, is one of the island's oldest buildings and offers insight into the island's defensive history. Nearby, the Church of the Assumption stands as a reminder of the religious and cultural traditions that have shaped the community. Small shops and cafés line the streets, giving you the chance to taste local pastries, sip coffee, or pick up handcrafted souvenirs. The area is also ideal for wandering without a plan, discovering quiet corners, hidden courtyards, and views over the harbor and coastline.

Practical details make visiting easy. The historic center is compact and best explored on foot. There is no entrance fee to wander the streets, though some sites, like the Torre del Conde, may have a small fee for entry. Most shops and cafés are open during the day, with a pause for siesta in the early afternoon. Parking is available at the edges of the center, but walking is recommended to fully enjoy the atmosphere. The area is accessible year-round, and mornings or late afternoons offer the most pleasant lighting and quieter streets for exploring.

Torre del Conde

Torre del Conde is one of the most important historical landmarks in San Sebastián de La Gomera and a must-visit for anyone interested in the island's past. Built in the 15th century, this stone tower was originally part of a defensive fortress designed to protect the town from pirate attacks and rival powers. As you approach the tower, you'll notice its simple yet imposing structure, standing as a silent witness to centuries of La Gomera's history.

Exploring Torre del Conde, you can walk around its perimeter and appreciate the architecture and stonework up close. The tower provides insight into the strategic thinking of the time and gives you a sense of how important the town was as a port and gateway to the Canary Islands. Though the interior is small, stepping inside allows you to imagine the lives of guards who once watched the coastline from its walls. Surrounding the tower, the small park area invites you to pause, take photos, and enjoy views of the harbor and nearby streets.

Practical details make visiting easy. The tower is open to the public most days, and entrance usually requires a small fee. It is located in the historic center of San Sebastián, within walking distance from shops, cafés, and the harbor. The area is easily accessible on foot, and visiting during the morning or late afternoon provides softer light for photography and a quieter experience. Comfortable shoes are recommended if you want to explore the surrounding streets along with the tower.

Visiting Torre del Conde offers more than just a glimpse of stone walls; it allows you to connect with La Gomera's history and imagine life on the island centuries ago. Standing near the tower, looking out over the town and the ocean, you gain a tangible sense of the island's past, making it an unforgettable stop in the heart of San Sebastián.

Church of the Assumption (Iglesia de la Asunción)

The Church of the Assumption, or Iglesia de la Asunción, is a striking historical and religious landmark in the heart of San Sebastián de La Gomera. Built in the early 16th century, it is one of the oldest churches on the island and reflects the deep-rooted Catholic traditions of La Gomera. As you approach, you'll notice its whitewashed walls, simple yet elegant façade, and the peaceful atmosphere that surrounds the church, offering a quiet escape from the bustle of the town.

Inside the church, you can admire its traditional wooden altarpiece, intricate carvings, and religious artwork that tell stories of the island's spiritual and cultural heritage. The serene interior invites contemplation and reflection, and the cool stone floors and high ceilings provide a comfortable space to pause and appreciate the history. The church also hosts occasional services and local religious events, giving you a glimpse into the island's traditions and community life.

Practical details make visiting straightforward. The church is open to the public most days, with free entry, though donations are often appreciated. It is located in the historic center, within easy walking distance from Torre del Conde, shops, and cafés. Visiting in the morning or early afternoon is ideal for quieter exploration and better lighting for photography. Respectful clothing is recommended as it remains a place of worship, and shoes suitable for walking on stone floors will make your visit more comfortable.

Visiting the Church of the Assumption allows you to connect with the spiritual and historical roots of La Gomera. Standing inside or admiring its façade, you gain a deeper appreciation for the island's cultural identity and centuries-old traditions. It is a peaceful and meaningful stop that complements the experience of exploring San Sebastián's historic center.

Archaeological Museum of La Gomera

The Archaeological Museum of La Gomera, located in the heart of San Sebastián, is a must-visit for anyone curious about the island's ancient history and its original inhabitants, the Guanches. The museum provides a fascinating insight into life on the island before European colonization, showcasing artifacts, tools, pottery, and rock carvings that reveal the culture, daily routines, and spiritual practices of the early settlers.

As you explore the museum, you will notice how carefully the exhibits are arranged to tell a clear story of La Gomera's past. The displays highlight everything from burial customs and ritual objects to everyday tools, helping you understand how the Guanches lived, farmed, and interacted with the natural environment. Interactive panels and models provide context for the artifacts, making the experience accessible and engaging even if you are new to the island's history. The museum also often hosts temporary exhibitions that focus on specific aspects of Guanche culture or local archaeology, giving repeat visitors a reason to return.

Practical details are straightforward. The museum is open most days, with standard opening hours typically in the morning and early afternoon, though it's best to confirm locally. Entrance usually requires a small fee, which contributes to the preservation of the exhibits. The museum is located within walking distance of Torre del Conde and the Church of the Assumption, making it easy to combine several cultural visits in a single trip. Comfortable shoes are recommended for walking through the galleries, and taking notes or photos is often allowed, though flash photography may be restricted.

Visiting the Archaeological Museum of La Gomera provides a deeper understanding of the island beyond its natural beauty. Walking through its exhibits, you gain a tangible sense of the people who lived here centuries ago and the rich cultural heritage that shapes La Gomera today. It's an educational and engaging stop that enriches your experience of the island's history and traditions.

Hermigua's Banana Plantations and El Pescante Ruins

Hermigua is a town nestled in a fertile valley on the northern side of La Gomera, and its banana plantations are among the most iconic sights of the island. Walking through the plantations, you'll see rows of lush green banana plants stretching along the terraces, reflecting centuries of agricultural tradition. The sight of the neatly organized crops against the backdrop of steep cliffs and misty mountains is both calming and impressive, giving you a sense of the harmony between human activity and nature.

While exploring the plantations, you can learn about traditional cultivation methods and the local economy, which has long relied on these crops. Small pathways and roads allow you to wander through the terraces and enjoy the surrounding views, offering great photo opportunities and a chance to appreciate the scale of these productive landscapes. Many local farms also sell fresh bananas and other fruits directly to visitors, giving you a taste of La Gomera's agricultural richness.

Close to the plantations, the ruins of El Pescante tell a story of the island's maritime and trading history. El Pescante was an old wooden crane used to load and unload goods from ships, standing as a reminder of Hermigua's past as a hub for banana export and other trade. The ruins offer a glimpse into historical engineering and the connection between the town's agriculture and the ocean. Walking around the site, you can imagine the activity that once took place here and the efforts required to transport goods across the cliffs to the waiting ships.

Practical details make visiting Hermigua simple. The town is accessible by car or bus from other parts of La Gomera, with parking available near the plantations and El Pescante. Both sites can be visited year-round, and there is no entrance fee. Comfortable shoes are recommended for walking through the terraces and uneven terrain, and bringing water and sun protection is advised, especially in warmer months. Visiting in the morning or late afternoon provides the best light for photography and a more comfortable temperature for exploring.

Experiencing Hermigua's banana plantations and the El Pescante ruins allows you to connect with La Gomera's agricultural heritage and maritime history. The combination of green terraces, dramatic cliffs, and historical structures offers a unique perspective on the island's past and present, making Hermigua a destination that is both scenic and culturally rich.

Agulo – "The Bonbon of La Gomera"

Agulo is often called "The Bonbon of La Gomera," and it's easy to see why. This small northern village sits on a hillside with terraced fields, colorful houses, and stunning views of the ocean, making it one of the most picturesque spots on the island. Walking through Agulo, you'll feel as if you've stepped into a postcard, with narrow streets, traditional architecture, and a calm, welcoming atmosphere that invites you to linger and explore.

As you wander, you can visit local shops and cafés, taste regional pastries, and interact with friendly residents who often share stories about the village's history and traditions. Agulo also offers access to hiking trails that take you into the surrounding hills, through lush greenery, and up to viewpoints overlooking the coastline. The village is particularly famous for its sunsets, where the sky over the Atlantic turns golden, creating moments that are perfect for photography or simply quiet reflection.

Practical details make Agulo easy to visit. The village is accessible by car from San Sebastián or other northern towns, with parking available on the outskirts of the village. There is no entrance fee to explore the streets, and most shops and cafés are open during the day, though a siesta break may occur in the early afternoon. Comfortable walking shoes are recommended for navigating the cobbled streets, and a light jacket may be useful in the evening when temperatures drop slightly.

Vallehermoso and Its Botanical Gardens

Vallehermoso, which translates to "Beautiful Valley," lives up to its name with lush landscapes, charming streets, and a relaxed atmosphere that makes it a joy to explore. Nestled between mountains and the ocean, this town offers a glimpse into traditional island life, with whitewashed houses, small plazas, and local markets that reflect the community's daily rhythms. As you wander the streets, you'll notice the care given to gardens, terraces, and public spaces, creating an environment that feels vibrant yet peaceful.

A highlight of Vallehermoso is its botanical gardens, which showcase the island's diverse plant life in a carefully maintained setting. Walking through the gardens, you'll see endemic species, exotic plants, and beautifully arranged displays that highlight La Gomera's unique flora. The gardens also provide shaded paths, seating areas, and viewpoints where you can pause and take in the surrounding valley and mountains. For those interested in nature or photography, the botanical gardens are a perfect stop to appreciate both the variety of plants and the tranquil atmosphere of Vallehermoso.

Practical details make visiting simple. Vallehermoso is accessible by car or bus from other parts of the island, with parking available near the town center and the gardens. Entrance to the botanical gardens usually requires a small fee, and they are open most days of the week, though hours may vary seasonally. Comfortable walking shoes are recommended, and bringing water or a light jacket can enhance your visit, especially during warmer months or cooler mornings. Visiting in the morning or late afternoon provides the best lighting for photographs and a more comfortable temperature for exploring.

Experiencing Vallehermoso and its botanical gardens allows you to enjoy the combination of natural beauty, cultural charm, and peaceful surroundings that define La Gomera. Strolling through the town, exploring the gardens, and taking in the views, you'll gain a sense of the island's unique character and its ability to blend human life with the stunning landscapes that surround it.

Playa de Santiago's Fishing Village Charm

Playa de Santiago is a small coastal town on the southern side of La Gomera, known for its relaxed atmosphere and authentic fishing village charm. As you walk along the harbor, you'll see fishermen tending to their boats, nets drying in the sun, and local seafood being prepared for the day's market. The town's calm streets, traditional architecture, and seaside cafes invite you to slow down, take in the scenery, and enjoy the simplicity of life by the ocean.

Exploring Playa de Santiago, you can stroll along the promenade, watch the boats coming and going, or visit small shops selling local crafts. The town also offers access to nearby beaches where you can relax, swim, or simply enjoy the view of the Atlantic stretching to the horizon. In the surrounding hills, hiking trails lead to viewpoints and hidden corners, giving you a chance to see the town from above and appreciate its peaceful setting nestled between the mountains and the sea. The local gastronomy is another highlight, with restaurants serving freshly caught fish and traditional Canarian dishes, perfect for a leisurely meal after exploring the area.

Practical details make visiting Playa de Santiago easy. The town is accessible by car or bus from other parts of La Gomera, with parking available near the harbor and main streets. There is no entrance fee to explore the town, and shops and restaurants are generally open throughout the day, though a siesta break may occur in the early afternoon. Comfortable shoes are recommended for walking along cobbled streets, and sun protection is advised for the beaches and promenade.

Visiting Playa de Santiago allows you to experience the authentic heart of La Gomera's coastal life. The combination of serene ocean views, charming streets, and friendly local atmosphere creates a memorable stop that highlights the island's maritime heritage and offers a peaceful retreat from busier tourist areas.

Monumento Natural de Los Roques

The Monumento Natural de Los Roques is one of La Gomera's most striking natural formations, located on the southern coast near Alajeró. This group of towering volcanic rock pillars rises dramatically from the landscape, creating an iconic and unforgettable sight. The rugged shapes and steep cliffs make Los Roques a favorite destination for photographers, hikers, and anyone who appreciates the raw beauty of volcanic terrain.

Exploring Los Roques allows you to enjoy both the scenery and the surrounding natural environment. There are several trails that wind around the formations, offering different perspectives and opportunities for hiking. From these trails, you can admire the contrast between the dark volcanic rock and the surrounding greenery, as well as glimpses of the ocean in the distance. The area also provides a quiet escape from busier parts of the island, letting you fully immerse yourself in La Gomera's natural charm.

Practical details make visiting Los Roques straightforward. The site is accessible by car from Alajeró, with parking available near the main trailheads. There is no entrance fee, and the area is open year-round. Comfortable shoes are essential, as the terrain can be uneven and rocky, and bringing water is advisable if you plan to hike around the formations. Early mornings or late afternoons offer the best light for photography and more comfortable temperatures for exploring.

Visiting the Monumento Natural de Los Roques is an opportunity to witness La Gomera's volcanic heritage up close. Standing near the towering rocks, observing their dramatic shapes and the surrounding landscape, you gain a deeper appreciation for the island's rugged beauty and the forces of nature that shaped it. It's a destination that combines adventure, scenery, and a sense of awe that stays with you long after your visit.

BEACHES AND COASTAL ESCAPES

Playa de Vueltas

Playa de Vueltas is one of the most inviting beaches on La Gomera, located in the town of Valle Gran Rey. This wide, black-sand beach offers a relaxing atmosphere and stunning views of the surrounding cliffs and ocean. As you stroll along the shoreline, you'll feel the gentle breeze and hear the calming rhythm of the waves, creating a perfect setting for sunbathing, swimming, or simply enjoying the natural beauty around you.

The beach is lined with small cafés and restaurants, giving you the opportunity to enjoy fresh seafood, local drinks, or a casual snack while watching the ocean. The shallow areas make it safe for swimming, and the wide stretch of sand allows families and visitors to spread out comfortably. Playa de Vueltas is also popular for water sports such as paddleboarding or kayaking, giving you options if you want to combine relaxation with activity.

Practical details help make your visit smooth. Playa de Vueltas is easily accessible on foot from Valle Gran Rey's town center, with parking available nearby if you arrive by car. There is no entrance fee, and the beach can be visited year-round, though waves can be stronger in winter months. Bring sunscreen, a hat, and water, and wear comfortable shoes if you plan to explore along the coastline. Visiting in the morning or late afternoon provides the most comfortable temperatures and softer light for photos.

Visiting Playa de Vueltas allows you to experience one of La Gomera's most picturesque and tranquil beach escapes. With its black sand, calm waters, and surrounding cliffs, it offers a perfect combination of natural beauty, relaxation, and local charm that will leave you feeling refreshed and connected to the island's serene coastal life.

Playa del Inglés (Black Sand Beauty)

Playa del Inglés is a striking black sand beach on La Gomera's southern coast, known for its dramatic volcanic landscape and relaxed atmosphere. As you step onto the dark sand, you'll immediately notice the contrast between the rugged cliffs, the deep blue Atlantic, and the golden sunlight reflecting off the shoreline. The beach offers a peaceful escape, perfect for sunbathing, strolling along the water's edge, or simply enjoying the natural scenery.

The beach is also a great spot for water activities. Calm areas of the sea are suitable for swimming, while more experienced visitors can enjoy snorkeling or surfing when conditions are favorable. The surrounding cliffs create a sense of seclusion, giving the beach a private and untouched feel, even during busier times. You can also explore nearby paths that lead to viewpoints overlooking the coast, offering fantastic perspectives of the waves crashing against the volcanic rocks below.

Practical details make visiting easy. Playa del Inglés is accessible by car, with parking available nearby, and it is also reachable by local bus routes. There is no entrance fee, and the beach can be visited year-round, though the southern coast is usually sunnier and warmer. Comfortable sandals or shoes are recommended for walking on the black sand and rocky edges, and sun protection is essential during the midday hours. Visiting in the morning or late afternoon provides softer light for photography and a more comfortable temperature for relaxing on the sand.

Experiencing Playa del Inglés gives you a true taste of La Gomera's coastal beauty. Its black volcanic sand, peaceful atmosphere, and dramatic surroundings create a memorable beach experience that highlights the island's natural charm and makes it a perfect spot for both relaxation and exploration.

Playa de la Caleta

Playa de la Caleta is a hidden gem on La Gomera's coastline, offering a small, peaceful beach perfect for relaxing away from the more crowded spots. The golden-black sand and clear waters create a charming contrast, while the surrounding cliffs and natural rock formations give the area a sense of seclusion and tranquility. Walking along the shore, you'll enjoy the soft sounds of the waves and the gentle breeze, making it an ideal spot to unwind and connect with nature.

The beach is perfect for swimming and snorkeling, as the calm waters often allow you to explore the marine life close to shore. Small rock pools offer opportunities to discover tiny fish and crustaceans, which adds a playful element if you're visiting with children. There are no large facilities here, which keeps the atmosphere natural and unspoiled, giving you a sense of privacy and a more intimate experience with the coast.

Practical details help make your visit smooth. Playa de la Caleta is accessible by car or a short walk from nearby towns, with limited parking at the entrance. There is no entrance fee, and the beach can be visited year-round. Wearing comfortable shoes is recommended for walking along the rocky edges, and bringing water, sun protection, and a light snack is advisable since there are no cafés or restaurants directly on the beach. Visiting in the morning or late afternoon provides the best light for photography and a more comfortable temperature for swimming or sunbathing.

Visiting Playa de la Caleta allows you to experience one of La Gomera's quieter coastal escapes. Its intimate size, clear waters, and natural surroundings create a serene environment where you can relax, explore, and enjoy the beauty of the island's coastline in a calm and unhurried way.

Playa de Santiago

Playa de Santiago is a charming coastal area on La Gomera's southern side, known for its peaceful atmosphere and picturesque setting. The beach combines volcanic black sand with small pebbles, and the calm waters make it ideal for swimming, snorkeling, or simply dipping your feet in the Atlantic. As you walk along the shore, you'll notice the colorful fishing boats anchored nearby and the surrounding cliffs that create a dramatic backdrop, adding to the beach's unique character.

The town of Playa de Santiago adds to the beach's appeal. Strolling along the promenade, you'll find local cafés, seafood restaurants, and small shops that give you a taste of the island's authentic coastal life. The combination of seaside charm and local culture makes it a perfect place to relax, enjoy a meal, or spend the day observing everyday life in a traditional fishing village. The area is also a starting point for short coastal walks or hiking trails that lead to viewpoints, offering elevated perspectives of the town, the ocean, and the cliffs beyond.

Practical details make visiting convenient. Playa de Santiago is easily accessible by car or bus from other parts of La Gomera, with parking available near the beach. There is no entrance fee, and the beach can be visited year-round. Comfortable shoes are recommended for walking along the shore and nearby paths, and sun protection is essential during sunny days. Visiting in the morning or late afternoon provides softer light, quieter surroundings, and a more relaxed experience for swimming and exploring.

Visiting Playa de Santiago allows you to enjoy a perfect blend of natural beauty and authentic coastal life. Its calm waters, scenic backdrop, and local atmosphere create a memorable experience where you can unwind, explore, and truly connect with the serene charm of La Gomera's southern coast.

Playa de Avalos

Playa de Avalos is a remote and striking black sand beach on the northern coast of La Gomera, known for its rugged beauty and natural, untouched atmosphere. Unlike the more accessible beaches, reaching Avalos involves a hike through dramatic cliffs and lush landscapes, which makes the journey as rewarding as the destination. As you arrive, you'll be greeted by a wide stretch of dark volcanic sand, the sound of waves crashing against the shore, and a feeling of solitude that is hard to find elsewhere on the island.

The beach is ideal for those seeking a more adventurous and peaceful experience. Swimming is possible, but the waters can be rough due to the Atlantic currents, so caution is needed. Sunbathing, photography, and simply soaking in the raw coastal scenery are the main attractions. The surrounding cliffs and rocks create natural lookout points, offering stunning views of the beach and the open ocean. This is a perfect place for hikers, nature lovers, and anyone looking to escape the more frequented tourist spots.

Practical details are important for visiting Playa de Avalos. Access is primarily by foot via a trail starting from nearby roads or villages, so comfortable hiking shoes and plenty of water are essential. There are no facilities, shops, or lifeguards on the beach, so you need to bring everything you require for your visit. Early mornings are recommended for the best lighting and to enjoy the beach in solitude, while afternoons may bring stronger waves and winds.

Visiting Playa de Avalos gives you a chance to experience La Gomera's raw and untamed coastal beauty. The combination of dramatic cliffs, dark sand, and the power of the Atlantic Ocean creates an unforgettable natural escape where you can immerse yourself in solitude, adventure, and the wild charm of the island's northern coastline.

Secluded Coves and Hidden Shores

La Gomera is filled with secluded coves and hidden shores that offer a quiet and intimate connection with the island's coastline. Away from the more popular beaches, these small inlets and rocky beaches provide an opportunity to enjoy the Atlantic in peace, surrounded by dramatic cliffs, volcanic formations, and untouched natural beauty. As you explore these hidden spots, you'll feel a sense of discovery, as if you've found a private corner of the island just for yourself.

Many of these coves are perfect for relaxing, sunbathing, or swimming in calmer waters tucked away from the stronger waves. Some of the more accessible spots also allow snorkeling, revealing colorful fish and marine life in crystal-clear pools. The cliffs and rock formations surrounding these shores create natural shelters, adding to the sense of seclusion and tranquility. These hidden areas are often connected by walking trails or small paths, which let you explore the coastline at your own pace and enjoy the diverse landscapes of La Gomera.

Practical details are important to make your visit safe and enjoyable. Most secluded coves require a short hike or careful navigation over rocky terrain, so good walking shoes are essential. Bring water, sun protection, and snacks, as facilities are usually nonexistent. There are no entrance fees, and the best time to visit is in the morning or late afternoon when temperatures are more comfortable and the light enhances the scenery. Always be cautious of tides and waves, especially at less sheltered beaches.

Visiting La Gomera's secluded coves and hidden shores offers a sense of adventure and serenity that you won't find in busier tourist areas. The combination of dramatic cliffs, quiet waters, and untouched landscapes creates unforgettable moments where you can fully appreciate the natural beauty and peacefulness of the island's coastline.

NATURE AND OUTDOOR ACTIVITIES

Hiking in Garajonay National Park

Hiking in Garajonay National Park is one of the most rewarding experiences you can have on La Gomera. This UNESCO World Heritage site covers much of the island's interior and is famous for its dense laurel forests, misty valleys, and dramatic peaks. As you step onto the trails, you'll be surrounded by towering trees, moss-covered rocks, and a canopy that filters the sunlight, creating a magical and almost otherworldly atmosphere.

The park offers a wide variety of trails suitable for different skill levels. Shorter paths let you enjoy gentle walks through the forest and reach viewpoints with panoramic vistas, while longer hikes challenge you with steeper ascents, rewarding you with breathtaking views over the island and the Atlantic Ocean. Along the way, you can discover hidden waterfalls, unique plants endemic to the Canary Islands, and the sounds of birds that are rarely seen outside the park. Each trail offers a chance to disconnect from the busier areas of the island and immerse yourself fully in nature.

Practical details make your hiking experience safe and enjoyable. The park is accessible by car or local transport from most towns, with several main entrances offering maps and information. There is a small fee for parking at certain trailheads, but access to the trails themselves is free. Comfortable, sturdy shoes are essential, and you should bring water, snacks, and layered clothing, as weather can change quickly in the forest. Visiting early in the day is recommended for cooler temperatures, clearer trails, and the chance to see wildlife at its most active.

Hiking in Garajonay National Park allows you to experience the lush heart of La Gomera. Walking under the canopy of ancient trees, listening to the sounds of the forest, and pausing at scenic viewpoints gives you a profound sense of connection to the island's natural beauty. It is an adventure that combines physical activity, discovery, and tranquility, making it a highlight of any visit to La Gomera.

The GR-131 Long-Distance Trail

The GR-131 is a long-distance trail that crosses La Gomera from one side of the island to the other, offering an unforgettable experience for hikers seeking both challenge and beauty. Stretching through valleys, forests, and volcanic landscapes, this trail allows you to see the island from perspectives that few other visitors experience. As you walk along the path, you'll be surrounded by lush greenery, dramatic cliffs, and occasional glimpses of the ocean, giving each section a unique character and atmosphere.

The trail is suitable for both multi-day treks and shorter sections, depending on your fitness and available time. Some parts wind gently through villages and farmland, while others take you through steep ascents and rugged terrain, rewarding effort with sweeping panoramic views. Along the way, you may encounter traditional hamlets, terraced fields, and hidden natural pools, each offering a chance to pause, rest, and immerse yourself in the local culture and scenery. The trail also connects with many other paths, making it easy to combine segments and create a hiking experience tailored to your preferences.

Practical details are important for planning your hike. The trail is accessible from multiple starting points, with maps and signposts marking the main route. No entrance fee is required, but good hiking shoes, layered clothing, water, and snacks are essential, especially for longer sections. Some parts of the trail are remote, so it's wise to carry a mobile phone, inform someone of your route, and check the weather before setting out. The best times to hike are mornings or late afternoons, when temperatures are cooler and the light highlights the island's landscapes.

Walking the GR-131 trail gives you a deep connection to La Gomera's diverse landscapes and natural beauty. Each step through forests, along ridges, and across valleys provides a sense of adventure, discovery, and freedom, making it a must-experience activity for nature lovers and hiking enthusiasts on the island.

Whale and Dolphin Watching Excursions

La Gomera is surrounded by rich Atlantic waters, making it an excellent destination for whale and dolphin watching. Taking a boat excursion gives you a unique chance to see these magnificent creatures in their natural environment, often swimming and playing just a short distance from the shore. As you glide across the calm waters, the excitement builds with every splash or leap, creating unforgettable moments and memories that stay with you long after the trip.

Excursions typically last a few hours and are guided by knowledgeable locals who share information about the marine life, including the types of whales and dolphins most commonly spotted around the island. You'll learn about their habits, feeding patterns, and the efforts being made to protect these animals and their ocean habitats. The experience is both thrilling and educational, offering insights into the ecosystem that surrounds La Gomera. The boats vary in size, from small, intimate vessels to larger ones with covered seating, allowing you to choose the style that suits your comfort and preference.

Practical details make planning your excursion straightforward. Tours depart from ports such as San Sebastián de La Gomera and Playa de Santiago, with booking recommended in advance, especially during peak season. Prices vary depending on the length of the tour and the size of the boat, and most trips last between two and four hours. Bring sunscreen, a hat, water, and a light jacket in case of sea spray or cooler weather. Motion sickness medication may be helpful if you are prone to seasickness. Early morning or late afternoon tours often offer calmer seas and better lighting for photography.

Joining a whale and dolphin watching excursion allows you to experience La Gomera from the ocean, giving you a sense of wonder and connection to its marine life. Watching these incredible animals move freely through the Atlantic is both humbling and inspiring, making it a highlight for visitors seeking adventure, nature, and unforgettable memories on the island.

Diving and Snorkeling Spots

La Gomera's clear Atlantic waters offer excellent opportunities for diving and snorkeling, allowing you to explore a world of marine life beneath the surface. The waters around the island are home to colorful fish, octopus, rays, and even turtles, all thriving in rocky reefs, underwater caves, and volcanic formations. Whether you are an experienced diver or a beginner, the variety of sites ensures a memorable experience discovering the island's underwater landscapes.

Popular spots for snorkeling include shallow coves near Playa de Santiago and Valle Gran Rey, where calm waters and accessible reefs make it easy to observe marine life up close. Diving enthusiasts can explore deeper areas along the southern coast, encountering dramatic drop-offs, hidden caves, and vibrant ecosystems. Several local dive centers offer guided excursions, equipment rental, and courses for all skill levels, making it convenient and safe to enjoy the underwater adventure.

Practical details help you plan your visit. Dive centers operate year-round, though sea conditions may affect certain sites, so it's advisable to check the weather and water conditions before booking. Prices vary depending on the type of excursion and equipment rental. Bring sunscreen, a hat, and a towel for after your session, and consider wearing water shoes for rocky entry points. Most excursions depart in the morning when the sea is calmer, providing better visibility and a smoother experience.

Exploring La Gomera's underwater world offers a completely different perspective of the island's natural beauty. Swimming among colorful fish, navigating volcanic formations, and observing the richness of marine life provides a sense of adventure and tranquility that complements your time on land, creating a well-rounded experience of the island's natural wonders.

Kayaking Along the Coast

Kayaking along La Gomera's coastline is a fantastic way to explore the island from a different perspective, combining adventure with stunning scenery. Paddling through calm waters, you'll pass rugged cliffs, hidden coves, and secluded beaches that are often inaccessible by foot. The rhythmic movement of the kayak allows you to connect closely with the ocean, while the gentle sound of the waves creates a peaceful and immersive experience.

Along the way, you might spot marine life such as fish, turtles, and occasionally dolphins, adding excitement and wonder to your journey. Kayak excursions often include guided tours led by local experts who can point out geological formations, natural landmarks, and historical sites along the coast. Whether you choose a short tour or a longer route, paddling gives you the freedom to explore at your own pace while enjoying the beauty and tranquility of La Gomera's waters.

Practical details are important for a safe and enjoyable trip. Kayaking excursions usually depart from Playa de Santiago or Valle Gran Rey, with rental options and guided tours available year-round. Life jackets are provided, and basic instruction is given for beginners. Bring sun protection, water, and a waterproof bag for valuables. Calm mornings are ideal for kayaking, providing smoother waters and better visibility, while late afternoon trips offer beautiful light and cooler temperatures. Some routes may require moderate physical effort, so consider your fitness level when choosing a tour.

Kayaking along La Gomera's coast lets you experience the island in a unique and active way. Gliding past cliffs, discovering hidden coves, and observing marine life up close creates a memorable adventure that blends relaxation, exploration, and the thrill of being fully immersed in the natural beauty of the Atlantic.

Birdwatching in Valle Gran Rey

Valle Gran Rey is not only stunning for its landscapes but also for the variety of birds that inhabit the valley and surrounding cliffs. Birdwatching here allows you to connect with the island's wildlife and observe species that are unique to the Canary Islands. As you walk through terraces, along the river, or near the forested areas, you'll notice small songbirds, pigeons, and occasionally birds of prey gliding over the valley. The peaceful environment makes it easy to focus on the sights and sounds of nature without distractions.

The valley's diverse habitats, from agricultural terraces to wooded ravines and cliffside areas, attract a wide range of species. Early morning is the best time to spot birds when they are most active, and carrying binoculars enhances your experience. Local guides or birdwatching tours can provide insight into species identification, migration patterns, and natural behavior, enriching your visit with knowledge about La Gomera's avian life. Even a casual stroll through the valley offers opportunities to pause, listen to the calls, and observe birds in their natural environment.

Practical details make birdwatching easier. Valle Gran Rey is accessible by car or bus, and the trails for birdwatching are generally easy to follow. There is no entrance fee, but bringing water, a hat, and sunscreen is recommended. Comfortable shoes are important for walking along uneven terrain, and a notebook or camera can help you record sightings. Mornings or late afternoons provide the best lighting for observing and photographing birds, as well as more comfortable temperatures for walking.

Birdwatching in Valle Gran Rey offers a serene and engaging way to experience La Gomera's natural beauty. Observing birds in their natural habitats, hearing their songs, and appreciating the variety of species adds depth to your understanding of the island's ecosystem, creating moments of calm, wonder, and connection with nature.

Cycling and Mountain Biking Routes

Cycling and mountain biking in La Gomera offers an exhilarating way to explore the island's diverse landscapes, from steep volcanic hills to coastal roads and forested trails. Whether you are an experienced cyclist or a casual rider, the island provides routes that challenge your endurance while rewarding you with spectacular views. As you pedal along winding roads and rugged paths, you'll experience the thrill of adventure combined with the serene beauty of valleys, cliffs, and the Atlantic horizon.

Popular routes include coastal roads where you can enjoy the ocean breeze, forest trails through Garajonay National Park, and mountain paths connecting villages like Valle Gran Rey, Hermigua, and Agulo. Each route offers a mix of terrain, including paved roads, dirt trails, and occasionally rocky paths that test your skills. Along the way, you can stop in small villages for refreshments, enjoy panoramic viewpoints, or take short detours to hidden beaches and natural pools. The variety of routes allows you to tailor your cycling experience to your fitness level and sense of adventure.

Practical details are important for a safe and enjoyable ride. Bike rentals and guided tours are available in main towns such as Valle Gran Rey and San Sebastián de La Gomera. Wearing a helmet, comfortable cycling gear, and sunscreen is essential, and carrying water and snacks is highly recommended. Some mountain trails can be steep or narrow, so a good level of fitness and basic mountain biking experience helps ensure safety. Early mornings or late afternoons provide the best conditions for cycling, with cooler temperatures and softer light for enjoying the landscapes.

Cycling and mountain biking in La Gomera give you a unique way to experience the island's natural beauty and challenging terrain.

Each pedal stroke through valleys, hills, and coastal paths offers a sense of freedom, adventure, and connection with the island, making it an unforgettable activity for outdoor enthusiasts.

WHERE TO STAY

Types of Accommodation

La Gomera offers a variety of accommodation types, each providing a different way to experience the island. Whether you are seeking comfort, adventure, or a closer connection with local life, the right choice can enhance your stay and make exploring the island easier and more enjoyable.

Guesthouses are a popular option for travelers who want a more personal and intimate experience. These small, often family-run properties are scattered throughout the island, especially in villages like Valle Gran Rey, Hermigua, and Agulo. Staying in a guesthouse allows you to interact with locals, get insider tips, and enjoy homemade meals that give you a taste of traditional Canarian cuisine. Prices typically range from 50 to 90 euros per night, depending on the season and location. Most guesthouses provide basic amenities like free Wi-Fi, comfortable rooms, and sometimes small kitchen facilities for preparing your own meals.

Hotels are ideal if you are looking for comfort and convenience. They are usually located near beaches, towns, or scenic viewpoints, making it easy to access attractions without long travel. Larger hotels often feature pools, restaurants, and organized tours, so you can relax without worrying about logistics. Prices vary widely, from 80 euros for budget-friendly options to 250 euros or more per night for upscale resorts. San Sebastián de La Gomera and Valle Gran Rey have several well-reviewed hotels that cater to different budgets and preferences.

Apartments and holiday rentals offer flexibility and privacy, perfect for families or travelers planning a longer stay. Many apartments are located in central village areas or along the coast, providing easy access to shops, restaurants, and beaches. They often include kitchens, living spaces, and outdoor terraces, so you can prepare meals, relax, or enjoy the views at your own pace. Prices generally range from 60 to 150 euros per night, depending on size, location, and amenities. Renting an apartment can make your stay feel more independent while still being connected to the local culture.

For those seeking tranquility and immersion in nature, rural lodges and mountain retreats are an excellent choice. These accommodations are often found in remote valleys or near hiking trails, offering breathtaking views of cliffs, forests, and the ocean. Staying in a rural lodge allows you to wake up surrounded by greenery, enjoy peace and quiet, and explore the island's natural beauty without the crowds. Prices range from 70 to 180 euros per night, and some lodges include guided nature walks or local experiences as part of the stay.

Popular Areas to Stay

La Gomera is a small island, but each area offers a unique experience, and where you choose to stay can shape your visit. From lively coastal towns to quiet mountain villages, each location provides different access to attractions, beaches, and local culture. Understanding the character of each area will help you select the best base for your stay.

Valle Gran Rey is one of the most popular areas for travelers seeking a mix of relaxation, natural beauty, and vibrant atmosphere. Located on the western coast, it is known for its terraced landscapes, palm-lined streets, and golden beaches. Valle Gran Rey offers plenty of guesthouses, boutique hotels, and small apartments, many with stunning views of the ocean. Staying here puts you close to beaches, restaurants, and local shops, making it convenient for both beach days and exploring surrounding hiking trails. Prices typically range from 50 to 150 euros per night depending on the type of accommodation and season.

Hermigua is ideal if you prefer a quieter, more rural experience. Nestled in a lush valley on the northern coast, it is famous for banana plantations, green landscapes, and access to the Garajonay National Park. Accommodations here are often guesthouses, rural lodges, and small hotels, giving you a chance to immerse yourself in nature. Staying in Hermigua allows easy access to hiking trails, waterfalls, and scenic viewpoints. Prices generally start around 50 euros per night for a guesthouse and can go up to 120 euros for lodges with special views or added amenities.

San Sebastián de La Gomera, the island's capital, is perfect for those who want a combination of convenience and culture. Located on the eastern coast, it has historic streets, restaurants, shops, and ferry connections to Tenerife, making it a practical choice for first-time visitors. Hotels and apartments here vary from budget-friendly to mid-range, with prices between 60 and 180 euros per night. Staying in the capital allows you to explore the town's architecture, markets, and harbor easily, while also having access to transportation for trips around the island.

Playa de Santiago offers a peaceful, authentic fishing village experience on the southern coast. Its small beaches, calm atmosphere, and seafront promenades make it ideal for travelers who want to escape the busier tourist spots. Accommodations here are mainly small hotels, apartments, and guesthouses, often with views of the sea or nearby cliffs. Prices range from 50 to 130 euros per night. Staying in Playa de Santiago allows you to enjoy local life, fresh seafood, and quiet mornings by the ocean, while still being close enough to explore other parts of the island by car or bus.

Choosing where to stay in La Gomera depends on what you want from your visit. Valle Gran Rey is lively and scenic, Hermigua is green and tranquil, San Sebastián offers convenience and culture, and Playa de Santiago provides peace by the sea. Each area gives you a different perspective of the island, allowing you to explore its beaches, villages, and natural landscapes in a way that suits your style and preferences.

Practical Tips for Booking and Choosing the Right Place

Booking accommodation in La Gomera requires some planning, especially if you want to enjoy the island without stress. The island is small and popular during peak travel seasons, so finding the right place early can save you both time and frustration. When choosing a place to stay, consider the type of experience you want, your preferred location, and the amenities that matter most to you.

Start by deciding what kind of environment you want. If you enjoy lively areas with restaurants, shops, and easy beach access, Valle Gran Rey is ideal. For a quiet, nature-focused stay, Hermigua or rural lodges offer peace and greenery. San Sebastián de La Gomera is practical for first-time visitors because it has transportation links and cultural sites nearby. Playa de Santiago is perfect if you want a tranquil seaside escape with a local village feel. Understanding what each area offers will help you select a base that fits your style.

Booking in advance is highly recommended, especially during holidays or summer months. Many guesthouses and smaller hotels fill quickly, so securing your accommodation early ensures you get the best options. Check online reviews, but also look for local recommendations, as some hidden gems may not be widely advertised. Consider the distance to the places you plan to explore, particularly if you will rely on public transport or prefer walking to nearby attractions.

Pay attention to the amenities offered. If you want to cook meals, look for apartments or guesthouses with kitchen facilities. For convenience, check for parking availability if you plan to rent a car, and confirm Wi-Fi access if you need to stay connected. Outdoor spaces like terraces, balconies, or gardens can enhance your stay, providing quiet spots to relax and enjoy the views.

Finally, consider your budget. Prices vary depending on location, type of accommodation, and season. Guesthouses and rural lodges are usually more affordable, while hotels and beachfront apartments may be more expensive. Planning ahead and comparing options allows you to find a place that balances comfort, convenience, and cost, ensuring your stay on La Gomera is both enjoyable and stress-free.

FOOD AND DRINK

Must-Try Dishes (Almogrote, Potaje de Berros, Fish Specialties)

Food in La Gomera is simple, hearty, and deeply connected to the island's traditions. Many recipes use local ingredients that have been part of Gomeran kitchens for centuries—cheese, gofio (toasted grain flour), fresh vegetables, and the fish caught daily from the surrounding Atlantic. Eating here isn't just about filling your stomach; it's a cultural experience that gives you a taste of how islanders live and celebrate. Some dishes are so unique to La Gomera that you won't easily find them elsewhere in the Canary Islands, making it essential to try them during your stay.

Almogrote

Almogrote is perhaps the most famous specialty of La Gomera and a dish that defines its culinary identity. It's a thick, creamy paste made from cured hard cheese, garlic, olive oil, and red peppers. Traditionally, it was a way to use leftover aged cheese, giving it new life with spices and peppers. The result is a tangy, slightly spicy spread that pairs perfectly with bread or potatoes. You'll often see Almogrote served as a starter in local restaurants, especially in traditional eateries in San Sebastián and Hermigua. A small plate typically costs around €5–€7, and it's usually shared at the table. Many rural guesthouses even serve homemade Almogrote with fresh bread as a welcome snack.

Potaje de Berros (Watercress Soup)

This hearty soup is another signature of La Gomera, a dish that showcases the island's love for fresh vegetables. Potaje de Berros is a slow-cooked stew made from watercress, potatoes, beans, pork ribs, and sometimes gofio. The taste is earthy and comforting, making it a favorite among locals, especially in the cooler northern valleys like Hermigua and Agulo. Traditionally, the soup is served with a side of gofio, which you can mix into the broth for a thicker, richer texture. A bowl costs around €6–€8 in small village restaurants, and it's a filling meal on its own. If you want an authentic experience, look for family-run eateries in rural areas where recipes have been passed down for generations.

Fish Specialties

Given its island setting, it's no surprise that fresh fish plays a central role in La Gomera's cuisine. Local fishermen bring in daily catches of tuna, vieja (parrotfish), grouper, and sardines, which are usually grilled or stewed with garlic, herbs, and olive oil. One of the most common ways to enjoy fish here is with mojo sauces—a red pepper-based mojo picón for a spicy kick, or a green coriander mojo for a fresher, herbal flavor. Along the coast, particularly in Valle Gran Rey and Playa de Santiago, seafront restaurants serve fish straight from the boat to your plate, often accompanied by papas arrugadas (wrinkled potatoes). Prices vary depending on the fish, but expect around €12–€18 per main dish. Dining in these villages gives you not only excellent food but also the pleasure of watching the sunset over the Atlantic while you eat.

Best Restaurants in San Sebastián

San Sebastián de La Gomera, the island's capital, is more than just a transport hub—it's also a place where you can enjoy excellent food that ranges from traditional Gomeran cooking to more modern Mediterranean flavors. Because it's where ferries and cruises arrive, you'll find a wide variety of dining options, from cozy family-run taverns serving hearty stews to stylish restaurants offering fresh seafood and creative takes on Canarian cuisine. Eating out here gives you the chance to experience the heart of Gomeran food culture in settings that are warm, friendly, and filled with local character.

La Forastera

Located near the center of San Sebastián, **La Forastera** is a small but charming restaurant known for blending local ingredients with international flair. The menu changes often, depending on what's fresh, but you can expect tapas-style dishes with a modern twist. The atmosphere is intimate, perfect for couples or small groups looking for something a little different from the traditional. Expect to pay around **€25–€35 per person** for a full meal with drinks.

El Pajar

Tucked away just a short walk from the marina, **El Pajar** is a family-run restaurant that specializes in classic Canarian dishes. Here, you can try authentic recipes like **potaje de berros** (watercress soup), grilled meats, and stews, all served in hearty portions. The setting is rustic and casual, with friendly service that makes you feel like a local. Prices are very reasonable, averaging **€12–€20 per person** depending on what you order.

Agape Bistro

For a more modern dining experience, **Agape Bistro** offers Mediterranean-style cuisine with fresh local touches. Dishes range from seafood pasta and grilled fish to creative vegetarian plates. The atmosphere is stylish but relaxed, making it a good choice if you want something a little upscale without being overly formal. A meal here typically costs between **€20–€30 per person**.

Bar Restaurante Caprichos

If you're looking for a casual spot to eat with great value, **Caprichos** is a popular choice among both locals and visitors. Located close to the town center, it serves a mix of tapas, fresh fish, and Canarian specialties in generous portions. The setting is simple but welcoming, making it a good choice for families or anyone looking for a laid-back meal. Prices range from **€10–€18 per person**, making it one of the more budget-friendly options in the capital.

Restaurante El Cañaveral

A little outside the busiest part of San Sebastián, **El Cañaveral** offers a quiet escape with traditional food served in a relaxed garden setting. It's well known for grilled meats, fresh fish, and house-made desserts. The location makes it a good place if you want to enjoy a slower meal away from the buzz of the port. Expect to spend around **€15–€25 per person**.

Seafront Dining in Valle Gran Rey

Valle Gran Rey is one of the most popular places to stay on La Gomera, and its seafront is lined with restaurants and cafés where you can eat with the sound of waves in the background. Dining here often means fresh seafood, local Canarian dishes, and international cuisine, all enjoyed while watching the sun set over the Atlantic. The atmosphere is casual and relaxed, with many places offering outdoor terraces that face the ocean. Whether you're looking for a romantic evening meal, a family-friendly dinner, or just a cold drink with a view, Valle Gran Rey's waterfront is the perfect setting.

Restaurante Abisinia

Located in La Playa, **Restaurante Abisinia** is one of the best-known dining spots in Valle Gran Rey. It serves a mix of Mediterranean and African-inspired dishes, with plenty of fresh fish, vegetarian options, and flavorful sauces. The terrace faces the sea, making it an ideal place to watch the sunset. Prices usually range from **€18–€28 per person**, depending on whether you go for a full dinner with drinks.

El Descansillo

Right by the beach in Vueltas, **El Descansillo** offers classic Canarian cooking with a focus on seafood. Their grilled fish and octopus are favorites, often accompanied by local mojo sauces and papas arrugadas. The setting is simple but cozy, and the ocean views make every meal more special. Expect to pay around **€15–€25 per person**.

La Salsa Restaurant

Located on the promenade near La Puntilla, **La Salsa** is known for its fresh fish specialties and international plates. The restaurant has an open-air terrace that gives you a direct view of the beach, making it a wonderful place for a slow dinner after a day of exploring. A meal with drinks usually costs between **€20–€30 per person**.

Charco del Conde Restaurant

Situated near the family-friendly beach of the same name, **Charco del Conde** is a relaxed restaurant where you can try tapas, pizzas, and seafood dishes while enjoying the sea breeze. It's a good choice if you're traveling with children since the beach is calm and shallow. Meals are generally more affordable here, averaging **€12–€20 per person**.

Restaurante El Palmar

On the La Playa stretch, **El Palmar** is a great place for enjoying traditional Canarian meals with a modern touch. Their menu includes grilled fish, meat dishes, and vegetarian options, all served in a warm, welcoming atmosphere. The ocean views from the terrace add to the dining experience. Prices usually fall between **€15–€25 per person**.

Village Tapas Bars

One of the most authentic ways to experience La Gomera's food culture is through its tapas bars. These small, welcoming establishments are scattered across villages and towns, each offering a warm atmosphere and a taste of traditional Canarian hospitality. Unlike formal restaurants, tapas bars invite you to share small plates, try a variety of flavors, and often mingle with locals. From rustic village taverns to modernized versions with creative dishes, they reflect both the island's culinary traditions and its laid-back lifestyle. Prices are usually affordable, making them perfect for casual evenings out.

Bar Restaurante El Faro – Vueltas (Valle Gran Rey)

In the fishing quarter of Vueltas, **El Faro** is a friendly tapas spot where the menu features freshly caught fish, octopus, papas arrugadas, and local cheeses. It's a relaxed place with tables both indoors and outside by the harbor, giving it a lively atmosphere. A round of tapas with drinks will typically cost around **€12–€20 per person**.

Bar La Tasca – San Sebastián de La Gomera

Situated close to the main square of San Sebastián, **La Tasca** is a cozy tapas bar that combines traditional Canarian small plates with Spanish classics like tortilla, croquettes, and jamón. It's especially popular in the evenings when locals gather for wine and conversation. Prices are usually **€10–€18 per person**, depending on how many dishes you share.

Tasca Telemaco – Hermigua

In the quiet village of Hermigua, **Tasca Telemaco** is a favorite among visitors who want a more rural dining experience. The bar is rustic with stone walls and wooden beams, and the menu includes local goat cheese with honey, grilled meats, and vegetable dishes made with fresh produce from the valley. Meals are affordable, averaging **€10–€15 per person**.

Bar Pedro – Agulo

Agulo is one of the prettiest villages on La Gomera, and **Bar Pedro** is a must if you're there. The tapas are homemade and hearty, often featuring stewed meat, garbanzos, and spicy sauces alongside cheese and bread. The setting is simple and unpretentious, with friendly service that makes you feel like a local. Expect to spend about **€10–€16 per person**.

El Tambor – Vallehermoso

Hidden in the northern part of the island, **El Tambor** is a tapas bar that offers both traditional and inventive dishes. Local specialties like almogrote and watercress soup are highlights, but you'll also find small seafood and vegetarian plates. Its peaceful setting makes it worth the drive. Prices are reasonable, around **€12–€18 per person**.

Local Drinks and Desserts

La Gomera's food culture wouldn't be complete without its traditional drinks and sweet treats. Both are deeply tied to the island's history, with many recipes passed down through generations. Drinks are often crafted from local ingredients like palm sap, grapes, and wild herbs, while desserts make use of honey, almonds, and tropical fruits grown on the island. Sampling these specialties gives you a taste of the island's authentic lifestyle, whether you're enjoying a post-meal digestif, a casual glass of local wine, or a simple slice of homemade cake in a village café.

Gomerón (Palm Liquor with Grape Spirit)

Perhaps the most iconic local drink, **Gomerón** is made by blending aguardiente (a grape-based spirit) with palm honey, giving it a sweet but strong flavor. It's often served in small glasses after a meal and considered the island's signature liqueur. You'll find it in village bars, restaurants, and local festivals. A glass usually costs about €2–€3, while a bottle bought from local producers ranges between €10–€15.

Local Wines

La Gomera produces unique wines thanks to its volcanic soils and sunny climate. The whites are especially well-regarded, often crisp and aromatic, while reds tend to be light and fruity. Vineyards in Vallehermoso, Hermigua, and Agulo supply much of the island's production. You can order a glass in restaurants for around €3–€5, or purchase bottles directly from bodegas for €8–€20.

Ron Miel (Honey Rum)

While originally more common in the Canary Islands as a whole, **Ron Miel** (honey rum) is also popular on La Gomera. It's sweet, smooth, and often served as a complimentary digestif after dinner in restaurants. You can usually get a small glass for **€2–€3**, or pick up a bottle in shops for about **€10–€12**.

Bienmesabe

One of the most traditional desserts, **bienmesabe** is a rich almond cream made with honey, egg yolks, sugar, and ground almonds. It's usually served with ice cream or sponge cake, making it both filling and indulgent. Restaurants often have it on the dessert menu for around **€4–€6** per serving.

Leche Asada (Canarian Baked Milk Pudding)

This dessert is similar to flan but firmer, with a caramelized top. Its flavor is delicate and lightly sweet, often enjoyed after lunch or dinner in family-run restaurants. Prices are usually **€3–€5** per portion.

Frangollo

A dessert made from cornmeal, sugar, milk, lemon zest, and spices like cinnamon. **Frangollo** has a creamy texture and a comforting, homemade feel. It's less common on menus than bienmesabe, but you can still find it in traditional village restaurants or during local festivals. Expect to pay **€3–€4** per serving.

Tropical Fruits and Palm Honey Desserts

La Gomera's warm climate allows bananas, papayas, mangos, and avocados to grow in abundance. These fruits are often used in simple desserts, sometimes paired with the island's famous palm honey, which adds a rich caramel-like sweetness. A plate of seasonal fruit with palm honey costs about €3–€5 in cafés.

ITINERARIES

One-Day Cruise Stop Highlights

If you're visiting La Gomera on a cruise stop, you'll likely arrive at the port of **San Sebastián de La Gomera**, the island's capital. With only a few hours onshore, the key is to balance sightseeing with relaxation while getting a true sense of the island's beauty and culture. La Gomera may be small, but its landscapes, history, and food traditions are enough to make a short visit unforgettable.

Morning – San Sebastián de La Gomera

Start your day exploring the historic heart of San Sebastián. Visit the **Torre del Conde**, a 15th-century stone tower built during the Castilian conquest, and stroll to the **Church of the Assumption (Iglesia de la Asunción)**, where Christopher Columbus is said to have prayed before setting sail for the New World. A short walk uphill takes you to the **Hermitage of San Sebastián**, which offers panoramic views over the harbor and coastline. If time allows, stop by the **Casa de Colón Museum**, which traces the island's role in Columbus's journeys.

Midday – Scenic Drive or Hike

For a glimpse of La Gomera's landscapes, head inland toward **Garajonay National Park**. If you're on an organized excursion, a guided tour will usually take you to **Mirador de Abrante**, a glass-floored viewpoint in Agulo with breathtaking views over the Atlantic and Mount Teide on Tenerife. Independent travelers can opt for a shorter hike in the park's laurel forests, which are cool, green, and atmospheric. These areas are UNESCO-protected and showcase the island's unique natural heritage.

Afternoon – Local Flavors and Relaxation

Return to San Sebastián for a leisurely meal before heading back to your ship. Order traditional dishes like **almogrote** (a spicy cheese paste) with bread or a fresh fish dish accompanied by local mojo sauces. If you prefer something lighter, many cafés near the seafront serve tapas and cold drinks. If there's still time, take a short walk to **Playa de la Cueva**, a beach just outside the port, where you can dip your feet in the Atlantic before boarding.

Practical Information

Most cruise stops allow between **6–8 hours** onshore. Taxis, rental cars, and organized excursions are available right from the port area. A guided island tour costs about **€30–€50 per person**, while taxis for shorter trips within San Sebastián charge around **€10–€15**. Walking around the capital is easy and requires no transport, but if you want to see Garajonay or northern viewpoints, joining a tour or hiring a car is the most efficient use of time.

3-Day Short Break

A three-day stay on La Gomera is perfect if you want to explore the island without rushing, giving you a taste of its landscapes, culture, and cuisine. You'll have enough time to visit historic towns, enjoy natural beauty, and experience local food, while also leaving space for relaxation. This itinerary balances sightseeing with leisure, so you can feel the island's pace and unique atmosphere.

Day One – San Sebastián and Surroundings

Begin your trip in **San Sebastián de La Gomera**, the island's capital. Spend the morning exploring the historic center, visiting the **Torre del Conde**, the **Church of the Assumption**, and the **Casa de Colón Museum**. These sites offer insight into the island's history, from medieval times to the era of Christopher Columbus.

For lunch, stop at a local restaurant to try traditional dishes like **almogrote** or fresh fish with mojo sauces. In the afternoon, take a short drive or taxi to the nearby **Mirador de Igualero** for panoramic views of the town and the coastline. If time allows, enjoy a gentle walk along the harbor or a nearby beach, such as **Playa de la Cueva**, to relax before returning to your hotel.

Day Two – Valle Gran Rey and Northern Villages

Dedicate your second day to exploring the western coast and the lush northern valleys. Begin in **Valle Gran Rey**, a village famous for its terraced landscapes, golden beaches, and vibrant atmosphere. Spend the morning walking along the seafront, visiting local shops, and perhaps taking a short hike to **La Calera viewpoint** for sweeping views over the valley.

In the afternoon, head north to **Agulo**, often called "The Bonbon of La Gomera" for its picturesque streets and flower-filled balconies. Stop at the **Mirador de Abrante** with its glass skywalk for stunning views of the cliffs and Tenerife in the distance. If time permits, visit **Hermigua**, wandering through banana plantations and exploring the ruins of **El Pescante**, the historic loading dock that gives insight into the village's maritime past.

Meals in these villages often feature fresh seafood, Canarian tapas, and local desserts. Valle Gran Rey has several seafront restaurants, while Hermigua and Agulo offer quieter, traditional options.

Day Three – Garajonay National Park and Departure

Your final day is dedicated to La Gomera's natural treasures. Spend the morning hiking or driving through **Garajonay National Park**, a UNESCO World Heritage Site. Popular spots include **El Cedro Forest** and **Alto de Garajonay Peak**, both offering incredible scenery and an immersive laurel forest experience. The park is well-signposted, and trails range from easy walks to moderate hikes.

After a morning in the park, return to San Sebastián or your base for a farewell lunch, sampling any dishes you may have missed, such as **potaje de berros** or a plate of tropical fruits with palm honey. Take a leisurely walk around the town or visit a small local market to pick up souvenirs before preparing for departure.

Practical Information

Transportation is easiest with a rental car, especially for reaching Valle Gran Rey, Agulo, and Garajonay National Park efficiently. Public buses are available but may require careful planning. Accommodation can be based in San Sebastián, Valle Gran Rey, or a combination of both, depending on your preferences. Daily meal costs range from **€15–€30 per person** at mid-range restaurants, while guided tours in Garajonay or organized excursions cost around **€25–€50 per person**.

5-Day Nature and Culture Tour

A five-day stay on La Gomera is ideal if you want to explore the island in depth, combining natural wonders, cultural experiences, and leisurely village strolls. This itinerary gives you a mix of hiking, sightseeing, local cuisine, and time to appreciate the island's relaxed pace without feeling rushed.

Day One – Arrival and San Sebastián de La Gomera

Begin your trip in **San Sebastián de La Gomera**, the island's historic capital. Spend the morning walking through the town's narrow streets and visit the **Torre del Conde**, the **Church of the Assumption**, and the **Casa de Colón Museum** to understand the island's role in the voyages of Christopher Columbus.

For lunch, enjoy traditional dishes like **almogrote** with fresh bread or a seafood plate with local mojo sauces at a seafront restaurant. In the afternoon, explore the nearby **Playa de la Cueva** for a relaxing beach stroll, then enjoy a coffee or juice in a local café while soaking in the town's atmosphere.

Day Two – Valle Gran Rey Exploration

Dedicate your second day to **Valle Gran Rey**, known for its terraces, palm trees, and lively village atmosphere. Walk along the seafront, explore small shops and artisan stalls, and enjoy a short hike to **La Calera** or **Mirador de Palmarejo** for panoramic views of the valley and the ocean.

In the afternoon, relax at **Playa de Valle Gran Rey** or **Playa de La Puntilla**. Stop at a seafront restaurant to sample fresh fish dishes or tapas while watching the sunset. Valle Gran Rey is also a great place to try local desserts and drinks like **bienmesabe** and **Gomerón**.

Day Three – Northern Villages and Garajonay National Park

Travel north to explore **Agulo**, one of the most picturesque villages on the island. Visit its colorful streets and the **Mirador de Abrante**, a glass skywalk offering spectacular views of cliffs and Tenerife in the distance. Then continue to **Hermigua**, walking among banana plantations and visiting the **El Pescante ruins**, an old maritime dock.

In the afternoon, enter **Garajonay National Park** for short hikes through the laurel forest, stopping at **El Cedro** and **Laguna Grande** for unforgettable scenery. This day combines village culture with the island's unique natural heritage.

Day Four – Adventure and Coastal Views

Spend the fourth day exploring La Gomera's rugged coast. Begin with a visit to **Roque Agando** for breathtaking views and a photo opportunity. Continue to **Los Órganos sea cliffs**, best seen by boat, for an up-close look at the volcanic formations.

In the afternoon, relax at quieter beaches like **Playa de Santiago** or **Playa de Avalos**. For a more active option, consider kayaking along the coast or a short cycling route to nearby villages. Evenings are perfect for sampling tapas in smaller village bars, giving you a taste of local life.

Day Five – Cultural Immersion and Departure

On your final day, revisit **San Sebastián** for any sites or shopping you may have missed. Stop at local markets for artisan crafts or souvenirs. If time allows, participate in a cultural experience, such as tasting Gomerón, exploring local music, or visiting a small winery in **Vallehermoso**.

Enjoy a farewell meal of fresh seafood or traditional Canarian dishes before heading to your departure point. Reflect on the island's unique combination of culture, nature, and relaxed lifestyle that you've experienced over the past five days.

Practical Information

A rental car is highly recommended for this itinerary, as it allows flexibility to reach valleys, villages, and national park sites efficiently. Public buses cover some routes but may require careful planning. Mid-range restaurants typically cost **€15–€30 per person** per meal, while guided excursions to Garajonay or boat tours to Los Órganos cost **€25–€50 per person**. Accommodation can be split between **San Sebastián** and **Valle Gran Rey**, giving you both central convenience and scenic coastal views.

7-Day Full Island Experience

A seven-day itinerary allows you to explore La Gomera in depth, giving you time to experience its natural wonders, historic towns, traditional culture, and relaxed island lifestyle. This plan is perfect for travelers who want a complete immersion, combining hiking, sightseeing, beach relaxation, and culinary experiences without feeling rushed.

Day One – Arrival and San Sebastián de La Gomera

Start your trip in the island's capital, **San Sebastián de La Gomera**. Explore the historic center, including **Torre del Conde**, the **Church of the Assumption**, and the **Casa de Colón Museum**. Stroll along the harbor and enjoy lunch at a local restaurant, sampling **almogrote** or fresh fish. Afternoon walks to **Mirador de Igualero** offer stunning views over the town and coastline. Spend the evening relaxing in a café or exploring the small streets of the town.

Day Two – Valle Gran Rey

Travel west to **Valle Gran Rey**, famous for its terraced landscapes and golden beaches. Spend the morning walking along the seafront and visiting the local markets. Hike a short trail to **La Calera viewpoint** or **El Molino Beach** for panoramic views. Enjoy lunch at a seafront restaurant with fresh seafood or tapas. Spend the afternoon at **Playa de Vueltas**, swimming, sunbathing, or taking photos of the cliffs. End the day watching the sunset while sipping a local drink like **Gomerón**.

Day Three – Northern Villages

Explore the northern villages of **Agulo** and **Hermigua**. Start with **Mirador de Abrante** in Agulo for dramatic views and the glass skywalk. Walk through the village streets, admiring the traditional balconies and flowers. In Hermigua, visit the banana plantations and **El Pescante ruins**. Lunch in Hermigua allows you to sample rustic dishes such as **potaje de berros**. Spend the afternoon walking local trails or enjoying a quiet café.

Day Four – Garajonay National Park

Dedicate a full day to La Gomera's iconic forest. Start at **Alto de Garajonay Peak**, then hike through **El Cedro Forest** for an immersive laurel forest experience. Stop at **Laguna Grande** to relax and take photos. Pack a picnic or have lunch at a small park café. Guided tours are optional but offer in-depth explanations of the park's flora, fauna, and geology. Return in the evening to your accommodation for a quiet dinner.

Day Five – Southern Coast and Playa de Santiago

Spend the day along the southern coast, visiting **Playa de Santiago**, a peaceful fishing village. Walk along the harbor, enjoy a seafood lunch, and relax on the beach. Take a short trip to **Monumento Natural de Los Roques**, impressive rock formations rising from the sea, ideal for photos. Explore small cafés or local shops for souvenirs before returning to your accommodation.

Day Six – Adventure and Outdoor Activities

Use this day for outdoor pursuits. Join a **whale and dolphin watching tour**, go **kayaking along the coast**, or explore **diving and snorkeling spots** if you enjoy water activities. Alternatively, try **cycling or mountain biking** along scenic trails near Valle Gran Rey or Hermigua. Lunch can be enjoyed in a village restaurant, offering both energy for your activities and a taste of local flavors. Evening can be spent sampling local wine or desserts at a small café.

Day Seven – Leisure and Farewell

On your final day, take it slow. Revisit a favorite village or beach, like Valle Gran Rey or Playa de Vueltas, for one last walk or swim. Stop at a small market or café for a final taste of local specialties such as **almogrote**, **bienmesabe**, or **Ron Miel**. Pack, enjoy a leisurely lunch, and reflect on your week exploring La Gomera before departure.

Practical Information

A rental car is essential for a full island itinerary, as it allows you to easily reach northern and western villages, Garajonay National Park, and southern beaches. Accommodation can be split between San Sebastián, Valle Gran Rey, and another village to minimize daily travel. Mid-range restaurant meals cost **€15–€30 per person**, while organized tours for hiking, water sports, or park visits can range from **€20–€50**.

Hiking-Focused Itinerary

La Gomera is a hiker's paradise, known for its rugged landscapes, laurel forests, dramatic cliffs, and ocean views. This itinerary is designed for travelers who want to explore the island primarily on foot, with trails ranging from gentle walks to more challenging hikes. Along the way, you'll encounter natural wonders, scenic viewpoints, and traditional villages, allowing you to fully experience the island's outdoor beauty.

Day One – Arrival and Light Orientation Hike

Begin in **San Sebastián de La Gomera**, where you can take a short walk around the historic center to stretch your legs after arrival. Visit the **Torre del Conde** and **Church of the Assumption** briefly, then head to a nearby trail such as **Mirador de Igualero**, which offers panoramic views of the town and coastline. This initial hike is gentle and a perfect introduction to the island's terrain. Evening is reserved for a relaxed dinner in town.

Day Two – Valle Gran Rey Coastal Hikes

Spend the day exploring **Valle Gran Rey** on foot. Start with the trail from **La Calera** down to the village, passing terraced landscapes, palm groves, and small farms. Continue along the coastline to **Playa de Vueltas**, stopping at viewpoints for photographs. Lunch at a seafront restaurant offers a well-deserved break. In the afternoon, take the short but steep path up to **Mirador de Abrante** for dramatic views of the Atlantic and cliffs.

Day Three – Northern Villages and Forest Trails

Hike through the northern valleys starting in **Hermigua**. Explore trails around the banana plantations and take the path leading to the

El Pescante ruins, an old dock used for shipping bananas. Continue on to Agulo, wandering through cobbled streets and small pathways that connect the village to surrounding viewpoints. This day combines cultural exploration with moderate hiking in verdant surroundings.

Day Four – Garajonay National Park

Dedicate a full day to **Garajonay National Park**, which is ideal for more serious hikes. Begin at **Alto de Garajonay Peak**, the island's highest point, then venture through **El Cedro Forest**, an ancient laurel forest with moss-covered trees and misty trails. Walk to **Laguna Grande**, a serene plateau surrounded by forest, perfect for rest and photography. Trails range from 2–10 kilometers, with options for both moderate and more challenging hikes.

Day Five – Southern Cliffs and Roques

Focus on the southern coast and the dramatic rock formations known as **Monumento Natural de Los Roques**. Hike along coastal trails that provide stunning views of cliffs plunging into the Atlantic. Continue to **Playa de Santiago**, where you can rest and enjoy a quiet village atmosphere. This day combines ocean vistas with light hiking and allows time to relax on the beach afterward.

Day Six – Adventure Trails and Water Activities

Mix hiking with adventure. Choose trails near **Vallehermoso** or **Valle Gran Rey** that are more challenging and less crowded, passing through forests, ravines, and small rural paths. In the afternoon, consider kayaking along the coast or joining a short whale and dolphin watching excursion to combine land and sea exploration. Evening can be spent enjoying a local meal or tasting **Gomerón** at a village tavern.

Day Seven – Leisure Walks and Departure

On your final day, take gentle walks along the beaches of **Valle Gran Rey** or **Playa de Vueltas**, revisiting favorite viewpoints and enjoying the scenery one last time. Stop at a café for a light meal or local dessert before preparing for departure. This day is intentionally relaxed to allow your body to recover from the previous days of hiking.

Practical Information

Most trails are well-marked, but carrying a map or GPS device is recommended. Proper hiking shoes, water, and snacks are essential. Guided hiking tours in Garajonay or the northern villages cost around **€25–€50 per person**, while self-guided hikes are free. A rental car is highly recommended to reach trailheads efficiently, and mid-range meals near hiking areas cost **€12–€25 per person**.

Relaxation and Wellness Retreat Plan

La Gomera is not only a destination for adventure and hiking; it is also an ideal place to unwind and recharge. With its quiet villages, secluded beaches, natural pools, and serene landscapes, the island provides the perfect backdrop for a wellness-focused holiday. This itinerary emphasizes relaxation, gentle exploration, and mindful experiences, combining spa treatments, slow walks, healthy meals, and breathtaking natural settings.

Day One – Arrival and Gentle Orientation

Arrive in **San Sebastián de La Gomera** and take a leisurely stroll around the historic town. Visit the **Torre del Conde** and **Church of the Assumption**, but keep the pace slow, enjoying the architecture and calm streets. Have lunch at a local café or restaurant, choosing light dishes featuring fresh fish or salads. In the afternoon, walk along the harbor and relax at a seafront terrace with a herbal tea or local drink like **Gomerón**. Evening can be spent settling into your accommodation and resting from travel.

Day Two – Valle Gran Rey for Calm and Sea Views

Head west to **Valle Gran Rey**, known for its laid-back vibe and terraced landscapes. Begin your day with a gentle walk along the seafront promenade, stopping at viewpoints like **La Calera** to take in the ocean panorama. Spend the afternoon at **Playa de Vueltas**, lying on the sand, swimming, or simply listening to the waves. Lunch in a beachside restaurant can include light, healthy dishes such as grilled fish, fresh vegetables, or tropical fruit plates. Evening meditation or yoga on the beach can help you fully relax.

Day Three – Spa Treatments and Village Calm

Dedicate the morning to a wellness session at one of Valle Gran Rey's boutique spas or wellness centers. Options often include massages, aromatherapy, or hot stone treatments. Afterward, take a quiet walk through the village streets, stopping at small artisan shops or cafés. Lunch can focus on local vegetarian dishes or smoothies made from tropical fruits. The afternoon is perfect for a slow coastal hike or sitting at a viewpoint to enjoy the sunset in silence.

Day Four – Northern Villages and Mindful Exploration

Travel to **Agulo** and **Hermigua**, two northern villages known for their tranquility and scenic landscapes. Walk through the cobbled streets of Agulo, enjoy panoramic views from **Mirador de Abrante**, and then continue to Hermigua to explore banana plantations and the **El Pescante ruins**. Meals in these villages are often simple but fresh, emphasizing local ingredients. This day is about gentle exploration, appreciating the culture without rushing.

Day Five – Garajonay National Park Serenity

Visit **Garajonay National Park** for a day immersed in nature. Walk through **El Cedro Forest**, where misty laurel trees and moss create a peaceful atmosphere, and stop at **Laguna Grande** for reflection and photography. Trails can be chosen according to your pace, with options for both short, gentle walks and moderate hikes. Picnic lunch amid the forest adds to the experience of disconnecting from the busy world. Evening can be spent relaxing back at your accommodation or enjoying a calm dinner in a nearby village.

Day Six – Coastal Relaxation and Water Therapy

Return to the coast for a day focused on the sea. Spend time at **Playa de Santiago** or a secluded cove, swimming, floating, or simply breathing in the ocean air. Optional activities include a gentle kayak ride or a short, guided snorkeling experience for mindful interaction with marine life. Lunch can be enjoyed at a small seaside restaurant, sampling fresh fish and local desserts. Finish the day with sunset meditation on the beach.

Day Seven – Reflection and Departure

Use the final day for slow walks, morning stretches, or a final swim. Revisit favorite spots in **Valle Gran Rey** or **San Sebastián**, stopping at cafés for light meals or a last taste of **bienmesabe** or **Ron Miel**. Take a few quiet moments to reflect on your week, capturing photographs or journaling before preparing for departure.

Practical Information

Accommodations for this wellness-focused itinerary often include boutique hotels, rural lodges, or wellness centers offering spa services. Rental cars are recommended for flexibility, especially to reach northern villages and quiet beaches. Healthy meals in cafés or small restaurants typically cost **€12–€25 per person**, while spa treatments range from **€30–€80**, depending on the service. Comfortable walking shoes, light layers, and swimwear are essential.

PRACTICAL INFORMATION

Money and Currency

La Gomera uses the **Euro (€)**, the official currency of Spain and the European Union. Understanding how to handle money on the island will make your trip smoother and help you avoid unnecessary stress.

Currency and Payment Methods

Most businesses on the island, including hotels, restaurants, and larger shops, accept **credit and debit cards**, particularly Visa and Mastercard. However, smaller cafes, local markets, rural houses, and some taxis may only accept **cash**, so it's advisable to carry a reasonable amount of euros with you. Coins are often necessary for small purchases, such as bus tickets or local snacks.

ATMs and Banks

ATMs are available in **San Sebastián de La Gomera**, **Valle Gran Rey**, and a few other towns, but they can be limited in smaller villages. Plan accordingly if you intend to travel to remote areas. Banks are open on weekdays from **9:00 am to 2:00 pm**, and some offer extended hours, but it is best to withdraw cash during the morning.

Currency Exchange

While most international cards work, currency exchange offices exist primarily in **San Sebastián**. You can exchange money at banks or dedicated exchange bureaus, though rates may vary. It is generally more cost-effective to withdraw euros directly from an ATM rather than exchanging cash from another currency.

Tipping and Local Practices

Tipping in La Gomera is appreciated but not obligatory. In restaurants, rounding up the bill or leaving **5–10%** for good service is standard. For taxi drivers, rounding up to the nearest euro or leaving a small tip is courteous. In rural guesthouses or for guides, tipping is discretionary and can reflect your satisfaction with the service.

Practical Tips

Carry a mix of cash and cards, and store them separately for security. Small denominations of cash are useful for markets, public toilets, and smaller purchases. Keep in mind that remote hiking trails or rural villages may not have ATM access, so plan your cash needs in advance.

Safety and Emergency Contacts

La Gomera is generally a very safe destination for travelers, with low crime rates and a welcoming atmosphere. However, being prepared and knowing local emergency contacts ensures peace of mind during your trip.

General Safety Tips

While violent crime is rare, petty theft can occur in tourist areas, so always keep an eye on your belongings, especially in crowded markets, buses, and ferries. When hiking in remote areas or Garajonay National Park, stick to marked trails, carry water, wear proper footwear, and inform someone of your route if going alone. Coastal areas are generally safe, but take care when swimming in waves or rocky spots, especially at less-populated beaches.

Emergency Services

For any emergency, **dial 112**, the standard European emergency number, which connects you to police, medical services, or fire services. This number works from both mobile phones and landlines.

Police (Guardia Civil / Policía Local): In San Sebastián and larger towns, local police stations provide assistance for lost items, accidents, or other non-medical emergencies.

Medical Assistance: Hospitals and health centers are located in San Sebastián, Valle Gran Rey, and Playa de Santiago. The main hospital in **San Sebastián de La Gomera** provides emergency care, while smaller health centers can handle minor injuries and illnesses. Pharmacies are widely available in towns and often open during daytime hours, with some offering limited night service.

Fire Services: Fire stations are located mainly in the larger towns, including San Sebastián and Valle Gran Rey, and can be reached via **112** in case of fire or accidents.

Travel Insurance and Precautions

It is strongly recommended to have travel insurance that covers medical emergencies, accidents, and hiking-related incidents, as some areas of La Gomera are remote. Keep a copy of important documents, such as your passport, insurance policy, and emergency contacts, both digitally and physically.

Practical Tips

Carry the **112 number** in your phone and note down the nearest hospital and police station for the area you are staying. Always inform your accommodation or local guides if you plan to hike or visit secluded areas. Basic first aid kits are handy for minor cuts, insect bites, or scrapes while exploring the trails.

Internet and Mobile Connectivity

Staying connected on La Gomera is generally straightforward, but knowing what to expect will help you plan your work, communication, and navigation while on the island.

Mobile Networks and SIM Cards

La Gomera is covered by the main Spanish mobile networks, including **Movistar**, **Vodafone**, and **Orange**. Signal strength is strong in towns like **San Sebastián de La Gomera**, **Valle Gran Rey**, and **Playa de Santiago**, but it can be limited in remote hiking trails, mountain areas, and some northern villages.

Purchasing a **local SIM card** is easy and affordable if you want data without relying on Wi-Fi. SIM cards are available at mobile stores in San Sebastián and major towns. Packages often include data, calls, and text options suitable for tourists. Make sure your phone is unlocked before trying to use a local SIM.

Wi-Fi Availability

Wi-Fi is widely available in hotels, guesthouses, rural lodges, and cafés. Larger towns generally provide reliable internet, while smaller villages and rural houses may have slower connections. Public Wi-Fi is limited, so do not rely on it for work requiring fast, stable connections.

Practical Tips for Connectivity

If you plan to use mobile data extensively, consider a prepaid SIM card with sufficient data. Keep in mind that hiking trails, national parks like **Garajonay**, and secluded beaches may not have any signal. Download maps, guides, or entertainment in advance if you expect to spend long periods offline. Power banks are useful for keeping devices charged while exploring the island.

Sustainable and Responsible Travel on La Gomera

La Gomera is a small island with delicate ecosystems, traditional villages, and a slow-paced lifestyle. Traveling responsibly here ensures that you help protect its natural beauty, support local communities, and enjoy an authentic experience without leaving a negative impact.

Respect Nature

The island is home to **Garajonay National Park**, laurel forests, volcanic cliffs, and unique flora and fauna. When hiking or exploring, stick to marked trails to avoid damaging plants and soil. Do not pick flowers, disturb wildlife, or leave trash behind. Use refillable water bottles, and carry out all waste to reduce environmental impact.

Support Local Communities

La Gomera's economy relies heavily on tourism, agriculture, and small local businesses. Shop at local markets, eat in family-run restaurants, and purchase handcrafted souvenirs rather than mass-produced items. This approach supports the island's artisans, farmers, and entrepreneurs while giving you a more genuine connection to the culture.

Responsible Water and Energy Use

Water is a precious resource on the island, especially in rural areas. Take shorter showers, reuse towels in hotels, and avoid unnecessary water waste. Turn off lights, heating, or air conditioning when not in use. These small actions contribute to the sustainability of accommodations and communities.

Respect Cultural Traditions

La Gomera has a rich cultural heritage, from the **Silbo Gomero** whistling language to traditional festivals, music, and crafts. Be mindful when visiting villages, participating in local events, or photographing people. Asking permission before taking pictures and observing customs respectfully enhances your experience and shows appreciation for local traditions.

Eco-Friendly Travel Choices

Consider walking, cycling, or using public transport whenever possible. Renting smaller, fuel-efficient vehicles reduces carbon emissions. Participate in guided eco-tours or volunteer for small conservation initiatives if available, which helps maintain the island's natural and cultural resources.

Practicing sustainable and responsible travel ensures that La Gomera remains a pristine and welcoming destination for future visitors. By respecting nature, supporting local communities, and embracing the island's culture, you create a more meaningful and enriching travel experience while preserving the beauty of La Gomera.

CONCLUSION

After exploring La Gomera through its villages, forests, cliffs, and beaches, you begin to understand why this island feels unlike anywhere else. Its slow pace, natural beauty, and friendly locals leave a lasting impression. Whether you came for adventure, relaxation, or cultural immersion, La Gomera has a way of drawing you in and inviting you to stay present in each moment.

Traveling here is about more than seeing sights; it is about experiencing the rhythm of life on the island. You will find that the mornings are soft with mist in the valleys, the afternoons are vibrant with ocean views, and the evenings are calm, perfect for reflection. From hiking in **Garajonay National Park** to walking along the terraces of **Valle Gran Rey**, and tasting local dishes like **almogrote** and **potaje de berros**, every experience connects you to the land, its people, and its traditions.

While this guide provides practical tips, itineraries, and advice, the real magic of La Gomera lies in exploration beyond the obvious. Wander down a quiet lane in a small village, pause at an unmarked viewpoint, or join a local celebration. Allow yourself the freedom to deviate from schedules and plans. These moments often become the most memorable parts of your journey.

Keep in mind that the island's charm comes from its balance of nature, culture, and simplicity. By traveling responsibly, respecting local traditions, and engaging with the communities, you not only enrich your own experience but also help preserve La Gomera's unique character for future visitors.

As you prepare to leave or continue exploring, remember that La Gomera offers more than just a destination—it offers an invitation to slow down, breathe deeply, and connect with the essence of island life. Carry these memories, lessons, and sensations with you, and allow them to inspire not only your travels here but also the way you approach new adventures elsewhere.

Do not be afraid to stray from the tourist routes. Some of La Gomera's hidden treasures—secluded coves, quiet hiking trails, and small artisan workshops—are found only by those willing to explore with curiosity and openness. Embrace the unexpected, and you will discover that the island's true magic often lies just beyond the well-trodden paths.

By keeping an open mind and a gentle pace, your journey through La Gomera becomes more than sightseeing—it becomes a personal connection with a place that is at once wild, peaceful, and profoundly welcoming.

Printed in Dunstable, United Kingdom